Know Your Rottweiler

D. Chardet

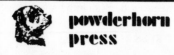

powderhorn
press

3320 Wonderview Plaza, Hollywood, CA 90068

ISBN 90 10 01903 9

Dick Chardet: Know your Rottweiler.
Publisher: Focus Elsevier, Amsterdam
Copyright 1977. Photos: Alain and Dick Chardet.
Drawings: Elly de Looff.

Sole license to translate KNOW YOUR ROTTWEILER by Dick Chardet into the English language and publish said work in volume form in the U.S.A. granted 1979 by ELSEVIER NEDERLAND B.V. to POWDERHORN PRESS.

Basic translation provided by Mr. John H. Macphail, England. Idiomatic and regional uses to Americanize that translation provided by Clara Hurley.

Cover photos: American, Dutch & Luxembourg
                    Ch. Quanto v.h. Brabantpark

Table of Contents

Introduction

Many dog lovers, who in daily life are reasonable and sober, lose their critical sense whenever they talk about their chosen breed.

If someone like that undertakes a breed monograph, the risk is that it will take the form of an interminable panegyric which resounds with the qualities of the breed in every key.

This is not that sort of book.

I have not attempted to write about the breed in a popular way, but to provide objective information. In so doing, more attention has been paid to behavior and the development of behavior than to the external appearance of the dog. Few pages are devoted to 'beauty of line, small ears, dark eyes and a noble bearing', although the warning against the so-called exaggerated emphasis on showing has led to more being said about this than was originally intended.

Baarn, August 1977
Dick Chardet

1. History

In the spring of AD 74, the quartermasters of the Roman Eleventh Legion laid out a temporary camp on the banks of a river in the south of Germania. In a short time it grew into a base camp. From here a network of roads was built which made it possible to open up the newly conquered territory and defend it by rapid troop movements. From this crossing point of important connecting roads the district rapidly gained in significance. The settlement which grew up here was called 'Arae Flaviae', the city with altars in honor of the imperial Flavian dynasty. Arae Flaviae became the capitol of a new province. Villas were built which were equipped with all the luxury which this period knew.

In AD 260, the Alemanni took possession, having driven the Romans out, and laid waste the city. Around the year 700 the ruler of this area had a Christian church built on the foundations of the old Roman bath house. Around this church a new settlement quickly developed. Like many old Roman sites, this one got the name 'Wil' (from villa). To distinguish this 'Wil' from others, it was called 'Rot Wil' from the red color of the roof tiles and bricks. From 'the Roman villa with the red walls and roofs' evolved the present name, Rottweil.

In the twelfth century Rottweil had become an important market town where, because of the importance of the cattle trade, a large group of butchers had established themselves.

From near and far buyers and sellers came to the great sheep, cattle, pig and also grain markets. The herds travelled from Hungary and France to Rottweil; the buyers and their dogs drove their newly acquired property far into the surrounding territories.

Driving a herd of cattle and keeping them together calls for a dog which is quiet, reliable and not too light. The butchers of

Rottweil bred such a dog themselves, the sole criteria being aptitude for working with cattle. The qualities of these dogs quickly became known and the foreigners bought them, too. They were reliable companions on long journeys and securely guarded the property entrusted to them This drover's dog was called the 'Rottweiler Metzgerhund' (Rottweil butcher's dog) or 'Rottweiler' for short. He carried far across the frontiers the name of his place of origin, the fame of his achievements and the prestige of his breeders. He was employed not only for driving cattle, but was also very useful for pulling the carts of farmers, butchers, bakers and pedlars.

After the donkey had taken the place of this draught dog and the driving of cattle with dogs had been forbidden by law, there was no longer any work for the Rottweiler. Numbers declined sharply, and in 1905 there was only one Rottweiler bitch left in Rottweil. But thanks to his good qualities of character, he had found a circle of adherents outside the butchers' frontiers, and through this the extinction of the breed was prevented.

About the origins of this breed there is little that can be said with certainty. In the eighteenth and nineteenth centuries butcher's or drovers' dogs were spread over the whole of Europe. Everywhere they were short-coated, brown, tan or black in color with white or brown markings. They were the last descendants of the medieval 'Hatzrüden' (boarhounds). These were robustly built dogs, often products of chance which displayed little unity of type. They guarded the farms and herds, and were used for hunting wild boars. They hunted by sight and were in fact a coarse kind of 'farmer's greyhound'. They were not bred at princely courts but by tenants, herdsmen and other members of the servile peasantry who were required to make a specified number of hounds available from time to time for hunting large game. The dogs had bells attached to their collars which made such a noise in hunting and fighting that the boars fled in panic and defended themselves less successfully. In Romance speaking countries dogs of this kind were called **Mastin, Mastino** and **Mâtin.** They had a mixture of the blood of greyhounds. hunting dogs, mastiffs and mountain dogs.

How mastiffs and mountain dogs came into Europe is uncertain. There is a striking similarity between all kinds of mountain dogs. They are distinguished only by differences in coat, caused by varied climatic conditions.

The mountain dog was extremely useful to man. He was protected by ancient laws. A law of the Alemanni from the seventh century prescribed a penalty of three soldi for killing a sheepdog which was capable of measuring up to a wolf. It was not until later that a distinction was drawn between a sheepdog and a mountain dog. Roman mountain dogs, to protect their throats in fighting, wore wide collars which were soft on the inside but equipped on the outside with rows of sharp spikes. Aristotle refers to the Molosser as a mountain dog and considers him to be a reliable companion who also renders good service in hunting. The Molosser was a descendant of the Indo-Assyrian dogs whose ferocity was feared, according to Aristotle; these latter were probably derived from the Tibetan Mastiff.

Curtius Rufus reports a lion hunt which took place at the court of King Sopeithes in the time of Alexander the Great. The fierce hunting dogs let themselves be torn to pieces rather than loosen their grip on the quarry.

Strabo in AD 25 says the same thing about the Tibetan dogs. Marco Polo describes the mastiffs of Tibet and says that they are 'as big as donkeys'.

In 1800 Samuel Turner, on his journey to Bhoetan, saw gigantic guard dogs, two of whom were guarding on their own a herd of several hundred yaks. Characteristic of the Tibetan Mastiff is his deep bark which is as sonorous as the sound of a gong. Compton, who owned a dog of this breed in India, speaks highly of their exceptional vigilance and their courage in fighting the leopards, bears and wolves which threaten the herds in the narrow ravines of the Himalayas.

Brook, owner of the famous 'Dsamu' relates that every year in October he became uneasy and 'went about growling for three or four weeks'; his instinct told him that the time had come for the journey south to the winter pastures on the India side of the Himalayas.

Dsamu possessed the original character of his breed; he accepted caresses only from his master, while with strangers he was unfriendly or even dangerous.

On the question of how the descendants of this large dog came from the Himalayas into southern and later western Europe, different theories exist. They are reproduced below.

1. Migrant peoples from the East, who occupied a high cultural level when the inhabitants of Western Europe were still going about in animal skins, brought dogs westwards with them. On warlike and trading journeys they came into the Indo-Assyrian culture zone. In the times of the empire of Alexander the Great and with the military expeditions of Xerxes, the dogs reached Ancient Greece. One of the breeds distinguished there was the Molosser, which resembled externally the present-day Komondor.

   The Molosser was mostly white with erect ears, a well-defined head and a noticeable ruff around the neck.

2. The descendants of the Tibetan Mastiff spread through Asia, and the peoples among which they turned up included Albanian tribes who then lived in the region east of the Caspian Sea. They migrated with their dogs along the Illyrian coast and later settled in Sicily and the southern part of Italy. The mountain dog of Campagna also took its origin from these dogs.

3. The Romans brought the Albanian dog from southern Italy and the Molosser from Greece. They served the Roman legions and fought in the arena. The campaign of Hannibal and Julius Caesar brought the descendants of dogs from the Himalayas into the mountain valleys of Europe. In the first century B. C., colonists took a light variety of these dogs to

Helvetia, while in the first two centuries A.D. the legions took both varieties with them. The lighter variety was used as a hunting dog, the heavier as a guard dog and fighting dog.

4. The heavier dogs of the European continent are descendants of the Celtic war dogs which guarded and defended the camp around the beginning of the present era. (The Celts held a great festival every year in honor of the goddess of hunting. On this occasion the dogs were wreathed with flowers, and master and dog took part in an enormous feast.)

These dogs were already present in Britain before the coming of the Anglo-Saxons, but it is considered unlikely that they were indigenous there. It is supposed that the Phoenicians brought the 'India dogs' from Assyria on their trading journeys, and that it is descendants of these dogs that are encountered everywhere along the Phoenician trade routes - the Mastino Napolitano in southern Italy, the Perro de Presa in southern Spain, the Bordeaux Dog in southern France and the Mastiff in England.

5. The Tibetan Mastiff spread northwards to the realms of the Huns. Their mountain dogs were descendants of the dogs from the Himalayas. When the hordes of Ghengis Khan penetrated into Central Europe at the beginning of the thirteenth century, they brought their dogs with them. In the track of the Mongol troops we find the successors of these dogs - the Oftscharka in Russia, the Kuvasz and the Komondor in Hungary, etc.

Little can be used of these theories from a scientific standpoint. The possibility that the mastiff-like dog is native to Europe is not ruled out. In London a skull has been found of a dog of this type from the Ice Age, while at Karlstein a comparable specimen has been found from the period around B.C. 700 (this dog must have been about 25½ inches in height); in France too there have been similar finds.

It is not inconceivable that mastiff-like dogs may have originated, accidentally or otherwise, in different regions. This may also account for the existence of pre-Columbian mastiffs among the Incas.

It is reasonable to assume that the short-coated Germanic fighting dogs had a common origin. A north European origin is suggested by the fact that the Gauls, according to Strabo, imported fighting dogs from Britain and that the Cimbri were accompanied on their expeditions by large pugnacious dogs.

The present descendants of the mastiffs give us a clear picture of the external appearance of the original mastiff types. Dogs in the past had to work for their keep. The poverty-stricken circumstances in which their owners lived resulted in the emergence of dogs that were tough and healthy and themselves did well on a very frugal diet.

It is clear that in such a situation a high degree of fitness for purpose was achieved; the type of dog was closely related to the work for which it was used. No large dog did the work that a small one could do equally well; every additional centimeter in shoulder height meant a greater requirement of food.

When one considers which breeds have contributed to the formation of the Rottweiler, it becomes clear that until the beginning of the present century the distinction between the various breeds was extremely imprecise. Different observers could well classify the same dog under different breeds.

A good example of this is a well-known fighting dog which in 1901 entered the ring against a (two-legged) boxer and was able to put this man on the floor. Some called the dog a mastiff, others a bulldog, and still others a bull terrier. The same applies to the dog that in 1892 'boxed' against James Odley in the East End of London, bit off his right ear and knocked him down. Even the shape of the skull can never be decisive in classifying dogs in breed groups. Discrepancies in skull formation can occur within a breed even where there is no mixing of breeds. Very broad skulls are sometimes found even in sheepdogs. From which I conclude that there is nothing certain at all about the derivation of the Rottweiler.

2. Pedigree Breeding and Development of the Standard

In the 'Sportblatt' of April 19, 1907, a dog fancier describes an encounter with a dog of an indefinable breed. It appeared - on the basis of 45 years experience with dogs - to be a cross between a Doberman Pincher and a short-haired German Pointer. The coat was smooth and black with tan markings. The body was short and compact, the ears small and drooping, the tail docked short. This dog had to be held close on the lead all the time because he behaved aggressively. The man was greatly astonished when he heard that the supposed cross-bred was a highly qualified Rottweiler. Now that a Rottweiler breed society has been formed, he is pleased to describe how the 'genuine' Rottweiler had looked at the first dog show held at Stuttgart in 1882.

With the present type, they had only color and coat in common. They were 27½" to 29½" high and showed considerable resemblance to a Mastiff, though the head was broader. The ears were large and triangular and set high. The body was inclined to be long and the tail was long and carried horizontally. The coat was fairly coarse. They showed much similarity to the Bayreuth butcher's dog, though the latter was even bigger and had cropped ears.

The short-tailed dogs which were to be seen at the Heidelberg show probably had Doberman blood; in any case, they did not look like the earlier Rottweilers.

The old butcher Wallenstein from Altenbusech in Hessen reacted to this in the same paper with the information that already in 1870 he had been using a black and brown dog to drive cattle and pull a cart. The dogs shown at Heidelberg in 1907 were exactly like this dog in appearance. He added that the Bayreuth butcher's dog could never have been used for driving cattle because a big dog was not suitable for that.

The evolution of the Rottweiler

1. Boarhound (Mastiff) of 1730.
After Buffon.

2. Cattle drover's dog of 1835.
After Reichenbach.

3. Cattle drover's dog on the coat
of arms of the Butcher's Guild of
Rottenburg,1870 (freely rendered;
in the original the dog has a long
tail).

4. Rottweiler of 1915, after several
years of pedigree breeding.

5. Rottweiler of 1930.

6. Rottweiler of 1950.

7. Rottweiler of 1960.

8. Rottweiler of 1970. Note the
relationship of depth of chest to
height at withers and body length;
also length of muzzle and shape of
skull.

In the period when the breeders and admirers of the Rottweiler were coming together in Germany, the appearance of dogs of this breed showed many variations in size, type of hair, skull formation and color of coat. The black and brown Rottweiler as we know him already existed, but also the all-brown with a brown nose, the blue with a slate-grey nose, the reddish tan with a black mask, the tan with a black mask, the coffee-colored with red markings, the all-red, the striped with tan markings, and the wolf-grey with black head and black and tan markings.

The beginning of pedigree breeding meant the end of a great deal of this variation in appearance; standardization was the watchword. With the rise of the show system competition began among all admirers of breed dogs to achieve a refined and noble appearance. Working qualities were forgotten and the dog had to be a pleasure for the eye. Beauty champions celebrated triumphs and gained a decisive influence on breeding. The first endeavor was to get rid as quickly as possible of everything in the appearance of the Rottweiler that was reminiscent of the hunting dog, including the characteristic amble which was thought unattractive. The backward turned, double folded ear could still find some favor, but not the half erect ear. Differences in personal taste, and the sound understanding by minorities who saw that the character and endurance of dogs were what mattered most, resulted in different associations concerning themselves with the breed.

In 1899 the animal painter Kull established the International Club for Leonberger and Rottweiler Dogs in an attempt to unite the encouragement of interest in both great Swabian breeds. This organization had little significance and soon faded out. In January 1907 the German Rottweiler Club (DRK) was set up in Heidelberg, and in April of that year in the same place, the South German Rottweiler Club (SDRK).

This latter association. whose standard stressed among other things the pincer bite, moderate angulation of the hindquarters, and endurance, was scarcely viable and soon merged into a third Rottweiler association, the International Rottweiler Club (IRK).

It is improtant for puppies to have contact with several mature dogs.

The police dog, *Rhino vom Krone,* AD 4013, ADRK working champion of 19

Rottweilers of 1930 and their owners.

Alc Zerberus VH III, ADRK working champion of 1968 (Assu Löwenherz x Ria von der Solitude).

An athletic Rotteiler of a type that is capable of great physical achievements: *Gerlach van het Brabantpark* (Moritz vom Silahopp x Ch. Burga van het Brabantpark). Behavior test in 1974: marked A.

A newborn Rottweiler.

A three week old puppy.

Both associations tried to set breeding on the right course, but they had different ideas about what was 'right'. Should the first aim of breeding be to achieve unity of type or to make no concessions in seeking to preserve, and if possible, improve character, even at the cost of external appearance? In the latter connection too there were differences of opinion - the breed standard makes this clear - about the size of the dog and the kind of undercoat.

These associations introduced a breed book. The DRK's first volume contained 500 entries (286 dogs and 214 bitches). In the unpublished second and third volumes, a further 485 were recorded. The pillars of breeding for the members of this association were *Ch. Rusz vom Brückenbuckel* (DRZB 1), *Ch. Ralf vom Neckar* (DRZB 2), a very lightly built dog with a great reputation for police service, and *Max von der Strahlenburg* (DRZB 48). The latter had a pronounced hunting dog expression; a long muzzle, little stop and very flat skull. Max, too, was an excellent police dog and played a great part in the official recognition of the Rottweiler as the fourth police dog breed in 1910, along with the Alsatian, the Doberman Pincher and the Airedale Terrier. Together with *Flock* (DRZB 49), he was employed by the Hamburg police and won first prize in various police dog competitions. The first World War, which he entered as a war dog, put an end to his career and his life. *Ch. Rusz* was much used for breeding. 20 per cent of the male dogs entered in the first DRK breed book were sons of his. The best known of these was the oustanding police dog, *LS Rhino von Kork* (DRZB 188).

The IRK laid the emphasis on breeding for show results and not on the breeding of working dogs. In this association they strove in the first place after uniformity of appearance and refinement of head type. With the DRK, the 'hunting dog head' predominated, whereas with the IRK they quickly disappeared.

IRK breeding was chiefly based on *Leo von Canstatt* (IRZB 29) and later on *Ch. Lord von der Teck* (IRZB 413), who brought the compact muzzle and broad head into the breed. *Leo* made his mark upon the initial breeding. The descent of almost all the 'great progenitors' and champions (with regard to external appearance) can be traced back to him. His most important son was *Garibaldi von Karlstor-Molkenkur* (IRZB 66) whose most important son was *Ch. Lord Remo vom Schifferstadt* (IRZB 130), a controversial dog on account of his height of 28 3/8'' (2 3/8'' over the maximum). The line continued with *Ch. Lord von der Teck* (IRZB 413) who fathered as many as 63 litters and was named as the first of the 'great progenitors'. The second 'great progenitor' was *Ch. Arko Terfwerk* (IRZB 955), the result of close inbreeding between *Lord* and his full sister *Minna von der Teck* (IRZB 411). *Arko* fathered 100 litters, his most important successor being *Cilli vom Filstal* (IRZB 1274) who, mated by *Lord Binder* (IRZB 1328) - a supposed descendant of *Leo von Canstatt* (IRZB 29) - produced among others *Fels vom Stuttgart* (IRZB 7471). From a combination of the latter with *Alma von Burgtobel* (IRZB 7547) was born, among others, *Alfon Brendle* (IRZB 12646) who was regarded as the third 'great progenitor'.

Not only the DRK and the IRK kept breed books; the SDRK also did so up to 1924. In addition, Rottweilers were entered in the 'Deutsche Hunde Stammbuch'.

Many Rottweilers in the initial period of pedigree breeding showed the swinging movement of the amble. It was especially long-backed dogs that did so (the short back is not flexible enough for this sideways movement). The long back was often weak and the angulation of the hindquarters was generally steep. The IRK intended to remove these faults by breeding a 'square' dog whose body length and height at the withers are equal.

In August 1921, discussion between representatives of the DRK and the IRK were brought to a successful conclusion; in the matter of the breed standard a compromise was arrived at, and the 'Allgemeiner Deutscher Rottweiler Klub' (ADRK) was established.

In 1923 the decision was to enter only black and brown Rottweilers in the breed book. Pedigrees were not granted to dogs of other colors. After the formation of the ADRK, subsequent breeding was exclusively determined by the beauty champions among the IRK male dogs. In 1924 it was decided to grant pedigrees only to demonstrably pure-bred Rottweilers. Their parents had to be already entered in the breed book at at least 18 months old at the time of mating. To promote vigorous progeny not more that 8 pedigrees were granted per litter. There was not yet agreement about prohibiting the use for breeding of Rottweilers with overshot or undershot jaws.

Between 1925 and the second World War concern continued to be exclusively directed towards appearance. The breed became even more 'refined' (shorter and more compact), the build more 'harmonious', the sinews and the ligaments of the joints firmer and the gait more attractive.

Long coated dogs were excluded from breeding. The undercoat, which in earlier times often came through to the· surface, was pushed back to the place where it was no longer visible. White patches on the chest disappeared almost completely. The carriage of the ears was improved and very light eyes hardly ever occurred. Excessive size disappeared, the throat became more clearly defined, and the square build superseded the longer form. The only thing which it had not been possible to do away with was the overshot jaw, earlier so often encountered in Swabia.

In 1943 one of the leading figures in the ADRK wrote that the war had shown that Rottweiler breeding was not what it had claimed to be; i.e., the breeding of working dogs. It was decided that with effect from January 1, 1944 the use of dogs for breeding would be limited to those selected on the basis of their suitability and value for breeding purposes. In this connection the absence of premolars would be considered a serious fault; one missing premolar would be overlooked in a bitch but none at all in a male dog. In future, dogs with unclear markings (black hairs among the brown) would be excluded from breeding. A bitch could keep only 6 puppies in a litter; increase in numbers merely for the sake of making money was not approved of. In 1948 the use of a foster-mother to rear a litter was prohibited - a well-meant but one-sided and narrow attempt to preserve one of the aspects of natural selection.

The standard has under gone quite a number of changes between 1883 and 1970. The first Rottweiler standard was drawn up in 1883 by Hertneck and Kull. This can be consulted in the book by Van Bijlandt (*'Les races des chiens'*). Some time later Strebel published a version of the standard which is reproduced with others in *'Doggenartige Hunde'* ('Dogs of the Mastiff Type') by Hauck. The establishment of the Club for Leonberger and Rottweilers prompted Kull to rewrite his original standard in 1901. In 1907 the DRK and the SDRK both framed their own standards, and the IRK followed suit in 1913. The amalgamation of the DRK and the IRK in the ADRK in 1921 led once again to a new standard. The ADRK revised its standard in 1960 and 1970. Hence nine standards were published in all.

The Standard of 1970

1. General Appearance

Rottweiler breeding aims at a powerful dog, black with well-defined mahogany markings, which despite a massive general appearance is not lacking in nobility, and is particularly suitable as a companion, guard and working dog.

The Rottweiler is a robust dog, rather above medium size, neither clumsy nor light, neither tall on the leg nor like a Greyhound. His frame, which is compact, strong and well-proportioned, gives every indication of great strength, agility and endurance. His appearance gives an immediate impression of determination and courage; his demeanor is self-assured, steady and fearless. His calm gaze indicates good nature.

He is very alert to his environment and to his master.

Size: Height at the shoulders -

Dogs 23 5/8 - 26 3/4''		*Bitches 21 5/8-24 3/4''*	
24 3/8 - 24''	small	21 5/8 - 22 1/2''	small
24 3/8 - 25 1/4''	medium	22 3/4 - 23 1/4''	medium
25 1/2 - 26''	large	23 5/8 - 24''	large
26 3/8 - 26 3/4''	very large	24 3/8 - 24 3/4''	very large

The length of the trunk from the breast bone to the ischial pro-
truberance should not exceed the height at the shoulders by more
than 15%.

2. Head

Of medium length, broad between the ears, the forehead line seen
in profile moderately arched. The occipital bone is well
developed, without protruding too much. The stop and zygomatic
arch are well pronounced. The length from the tip of the nose to
the corner of the eye should not exceed that of the upper part of
the head from the corner of the eye to the occipital bone.

Scalp: Tightly drawn all over, only forming slight wrinkles when
the dog is extremely alert. The aim is a head without wrinkles.

Lips: Black, lying close, corners of the mouth closed.

Nose: The bridge of the nose is straight, broad at the root and
moderately tapering. Tip of the nose well developed, broad rather
than round, with relatively large nostrils and always black in
color.

Eyes: Medium-size, almond-shaped and dark brown in color,
with well fitting eyelids.

Ears: As small as possible, pendant, triangular, set well apart and
high. When the ears are well placed and laid forward, the skull appears broader.

Teeth: Strong and complete (42 teeth). The upper incisors bite
scissors-wise in front of those in the lower jaw.

3. Neck

Powerful, moderately long, well-muscled, with a slightly arched
line rising from the shoulders; dry, without dewlap or loose skin.

4. Trunk

Roomy, broad and deep chest, with a well-developed forechest and well-sprung ribs. Back straight, powerful and firm. Loins short, powerful and deep. Flanks not drawn up. Croup broad, of medium length and slightly rounded, neither straight nor too sloping.

5. Tail

Carried horizontally, short and strong. Must be docked if too long at birth.

6. Forequarters

Shoulders long and well set. The upper arm lies well against the body, but not too tightly. Lower arm strongly developed and muscular. Pasterns slightly springy, strong, not steep. Feet round, very compact and arched. Pads hard, nails short, black and strong.

The forelegs, seen from the front, are straight and not set too close together. The lower arms, seen from the side, are straight. The shoulders should have a lay-back of about 45°; the angle between the shoulder blade and the upper arm is about 115°.

7. Hindquarters

Upper thigh fairly long, broad and well muscled. Lower thigh long, powerful, sinewy, broadly muscled, leading to a powerful hock, well angulated, not steep.

The back feet are somewhat longer than the front feet, equally compact and arched, with strong toes and without dewclaws. Seen from behind, the back legs are straight and not set too close. In a natural stance, the upper thigh and hipbone, upper thigh and lower thigh, and lower thigh and metatarsus form obtuse angles. The slope of the hipbone is about 20-30°.

8. Movement

The Rottweiler is a trotter. In this gait, he conveys the impression of strength, endurance and determination. The back stays firm and relatively still. The motion is harmonious, steady, powerful and unhindered with a good length of stride.

9. Coat

Consists of outer coat and undercoat. The former is bristly, of medium length, coarse, dense and lying close. The undercoat must not show through the outer coat. The hair is somewhat longer on both front and hind legs.

The color is black with well-defined markings of a rich, red-brown color on the cheeks, muzzle, throat, chest and legs, as well as over the eyes and under the tail.

10. Character

The character of the Rottweiler consists of the sum of all the inherited and acquired physical and mental attributes, qualities and abilities, which determine and regulate his relationship to the environment.

With regard to his mental make-up, his disposition is basically friendly and peaceful; he is faithful, obedient and willing to work. His temperament, his drive for action and for moving about are moderate. His reaction to disagreeable stimuli is tough, fearless and assured.

His sense organs are appropriately developed. His emotions are readily evoked, and his learning capacity is excellent. He is a strong, well-balanced type of a dog. Because of his unsuspicious nature, moderate sharpness and high self-confidence, he reacts quietly and without haste to environmental influences. When threatened, however, he goes into action immediately because of his highly developed fighting and protection instincts. Faced with painful experiences, he holds his ground, fearless and unflinching. When the threat passes, his fighting mood subsides relatively quickly and changes to a peaceful one.

Among his other good qualities are: A strong attachment to his home and a constant readiness to defend it; he is very willing to retrieve and has a good capacity for tracking; he has considerable endurance, likes the water, and is fond of children. He does not have a well-developed hunting instinct.

In more detail, the following instincts and character attributes are considered desirable:

a. *In daily life:*

Self-confidence	High
Fearlessness	High
Temperament	Medium
Endurance	High
Mobility and Activity	Medium
Alertness	High
Tractability	Medium-high
Mistrust	Low-medium
Sharpness	Low-medium

b. *As companion, guard and working dog:*
All the qualities named under "a", as well as

Courage	Very high
Fighting instinct	Very high
Protection instinct	Very high
Hardness	High

c. *Guarding characteristics:*

Watchfulness	Medium
Threshold of excitability	Medium

d. *Aptitude for nose work:*

Searching instinct	Medium
Tracking instinct	High
Willingness to retrieve	Medium-high

It should be noted that these instincts and qualities may be present in varying degrees of intensity, and that they often merge into one another and are inter-related. They must, however, be present as highly developed as is necessary for working efficiency.

11. Appearance and Working Faults

Appearance faults are noticeable deviations from the features described in the Standard. They lessen the working value of the dog only to a limited degree, but they can obscure and distort the typical image of the breed. Appearance faults, according to the breed Standard, include the following:

Light, tall, Greyhound-like in general appearance; too long, too short, narrow body; prominent occipital bone; hound-like head and expression; narrow, light, too short, too long, or coarse head; flat forehead (little or no stop); narrow lower jaw; long or pointed muzzle; cheeks too protruding; ram's or split nose, bridge of nose dished or sloping; tip of nose light or spotted; open, pink or spotted lips, corners of the mouth open; distemper teeth; wrinkles on the head; ears set too low, large, long, floppy, turned back, not lying close, or irregularly carried; light (yellow) eyes, or a light and a dark eye, open, deep-set, too full, round, staring eyes, piercing gaze; neck too long, thin weak-muscled, dew-laps or loose skin on the throat; forelegs set narrow or not straight; light nails; tail set too high or too low; coat soft, too short or too long, curly coat, absence of undercoat; markings of the wrong color, poorly defined or too extensive; white spots, dewclaws on the hindlegs.

More serious than the faults mentioned above are those deviations from the ideal which affect both the appearance of the dog and its working qualities. They are called working faults and are listed in the Standard as follows:

Weak bones and musculature, steep shoulders, deficient elbow articulation; too long, too short, or steep upper arm; weak or steep pasterns; splay feet; flat feet or excessively arched toes, stunted toes; flat ribcage, barrel chest, pigeon breast; back too long, weak, sway or roach; croup too short, too straight, too long or too steep; too heavy, unwieldy body; hindlegs flat-shanked, sickle-hocked, cow-hocked or bow-legged; joints too narrowly or too widely angled.

Excluded from judging and breeding are:

1. Dogs lacking one or both testicles. Both testicles must be well-developed and clearly visible in the scrotum.

2. All Rottweilers showing an abnormality in the hip joint. The

degree of abnormality leading to disqualification, and the measures to be taken by breeders are set forth by the Breeding Committee.

3. All Rottweilers with faulty bites and dentition; i.e., overshot, undershot, and missing premolars or molars (xrays are not accepted as proof of complete dentition).

4. All Rottweilers with loose or rolled-in eyelids (entropion) as well as those with open eyelids (ectropion). In case of doubt, veterinary examination is recommended when a dog with eye trouble is presented at a breed show or breeding eligibility test. The judge is responsible for sending information about the dog in question to the Studbook Office. If the trouble is still present when the dog is shown again, or if the eyelids have been operated on, the dog is forever banned from breeding. Concealment of an eye operation is a deceitful practice condemned by the show regulations.

5. All Rottweilers with yellow eyes, hawk eyes, staring expression or with eyes of different colors.

6. All Rottweilers with pronounced reversal of sexual characteristics (bitchy dogs, doggy bitches).

7. All timid, cowardly, gunshy, vicious, excessively mistrustful and nervous Rottweilers, as well as those of stupid expression and behavior. Dogs which show obvious laziness, unusually slow reactions or extreme one-sidedness in their character should be watched and examined with particular care before they are used for breeding (the possibility of deafness should be considered).

8. Decidedly long-coated or curly-coated Rottweilers. Smoothcoated or short-coated dogs with an absence of undercoat should be used for breeding only with the permission of the chief breed warden.

Running gear and gaits: The hindquarters are the means of support and act as a leverage for locomotion. In every type of action the forward thrust proceeds from the hindquarters, which are more strongly angulated and have more powerful and complex muscles than the forequarters. In conformity with the greater strain placed on them, the forequarters show a less angled system for support and braking. The propulsive forces are transmitted to the forequarters through the trunk.

The back plays an essential part in the forward movement, the powerful extensor muscles of the neck and back cooperating with the lower neck muscles, as well as with those of the inside thigh and stomach. Extremely strong and well-developed back muscles are essential for a good and enduring gait.

The types of gait in the Rottweiler are the walk, the trot, the pace, the gallop and the leap.

In the trot, the forequarters and hindquarters are mutually synchronized (brace, lift, float, support). The back remains relatively stable. In the walk, the back movements are more visible; in the pace (simultaneous advance of the hind and front limbs on one side), they are more pronounced and strongest of all in the gallop, when the back is arched like a spring and throws the body forward.

Faulty types of gaits are: Stiff, constrained, too high or dragging the ground, short steps, rocking, swaying, rolling, weaving.
General comments on external appearance: Defects in harmony (balance) and firmness of physique detract from a dog's appearance and working ability.

A dog's working usefulness depends essentially on his ability to move and run, and these factors, therefore, receive particular attention in assessing the appearance and character. There are several references in the Standard to the importance of the length and power of the limbs, back and shoulders, of the angulation of the joints, and of the muscles.

In judging a living thing, many imponderable factors also play a part, which can only be correctly appreciated in the total context by the trained eye of an experienced judge.

A few figures may be mentioned for guidance: A Rottweiler, which is 25 1/2 inches high at the withers, should measure about 29 1/2 inches from the breast-bone to the ischium. The chest circumference should be about equal to the height at the withers plus 8 inches. The chest depth should be neither more, nor very much less, than 50% of the height at the withers.

So much for the A.D.R.K Standard of 1970.

Comparison of the Standards

In the 1883 standard by Kull and Hertneck (referred to hereafter as KH 1883) and in that by Strebel (Str.) the height and weight of the ideal Rottweiler are given as 23 5/8 inches and 66.14 pounds and as 19 3/4 - 23 5/8 inches and 55.11 - 66.14 pounds respectively. In the other standards the height varies between 21 5/8 - 26 inches (DRK 1907); 21 5/8 - 27 1/2 inches (SDRK 1907); 21 5/8 - 25 1/2 inches (IRK 1913); 21 5/8 - 26 3/4 inches (ADRK 1921); 21 5/8 - 26 inches (ADRK 1960) and 21 5/8 - 26 3/4 inches (ADRK 1970). The weight is not specified in the later series of standards The weight of present-day Rottweilers differs from about 77.16 - 99. 21 pounds for bitches and about 99.21 - 121.25 pounds for males. Show champions among male dogs weighing 132.28 pounds are however not exceptional. There have been a good many changes in the approved ratios of length, height and depth of body though this may not appear at first sight from the measurements specified.

Kull 1901 consideres a "square" dog to be desirable, and so do IRK 1913 and ADRK 1921. ADRK 1960 speaks of 9:10 ratio of height to length. A dog with a height of 25 1/2 inches should be a little more that 28 3/8 inches in length. From ADRK 1970 a ratio 10:11.5 can be inferred in this connection; i.e., that a Rottweiler with a height of 25 1/2 inches should have a length of really 29 1/2 inches.

The ratio of height to length specified in the standard has thus been altered over the years from 1:1 to 1:1.11 and then to 1:1.15. This implies a marked increase in the body length. It must not be assumed that ideas about the ideal representative of the breed have changed and that the ratios in the standard have been altered accordingly, but rather that an adjustment to reality has taken place. The constant striving by selective breeding for dogs with a broad and deep chest and deep flanks has created unfortunately a longer dog which, so far as build is concerned, is moving in the direction of the present Bordeaux Mastiff.

The depth of loins evolved from "loins lightly raised" (Kull 1901) to "flanks scarcely raised" (ADRK 1921) and "flanks not raised" (ADRK 1960 and 1970). With an equivalent depth of chest this should not matter so much in the general appearance. With the pronounced increase in the depth of chest it has led to a radical change.

The head, where mentioned in the standards, was said to be of medium length. IRK 1913 and ADRK 1921 state that the back of the nose should not be longer than the forehead. ADRK 1970 indicates that both should be of equal length. Here too it looks as though there has been no change. This is, however, an illusion; because of the enormous increase in skull size, the vaulting of the skull and the so-called "stop", a completely different type of head has emerged. The differences between Rottweilers in photographs taken in 1910 and those of 1960 and later are very great. In addition, it was found some years ago on measuring the heads of 25 typical male Rottweilers that the average muzzle length was 3 1/2 inches and the average skull length 5 7/8 inches. The ratio of muzzle to skull was therefore 3:5 rather than 1:1. With an equivalent total head length of 9 1/2 inches, the muzzle has dropped from about 4 3/4 inches to 3 1/2 inches while the skull length has increased from about 4 3/4 inches to 5 7/8 inches.

So far as the teeth are concerned, it is striking in ADRK 1907 that then the pincer bite is regarded as ideal. The other standards make it clear that they look for a shearing bite and merely tolerate the pincer bite. The standard of 1960 expresses for the first time the

stricter attitude with regard to missing premolars; the teeth are required to be complete. ADRK 1970 repeats this.

There are changes too in the description of the ears; from "small"
or "medium-sized" and "set high and far apart", we finally have
"small and drooping".

Kull's standard of 1901 even spoke of high-set ears resembling
those of the present-day Fox Terrier. This standard also describes
how the long undocked tail should look and be carried. The
others recognize only the docked tail or the tail which is short at
birth. Kull 1901, so far as angulation is concerned, gives a picture
which corresponds most to the original shape of the Rottweiler in
his former occupation of driving cattle. Both the front and the
rear angulation should be steep. ADRK 1907 speaks of moderately angled hindquarters, while the other standards merely refer to
"good angulation".

30

3. Discussion of the standard

If we compare the present Rottweiler, as far as external appearance is concerned, with the original working dogs, we find considerable differences. The watch dog brought with them by the Romans to guard gates and encampments had the build, the size and the skull-type of the present German Pointer. The dog used by the Romans to drive and control cattle was smaller and lighter. Of the boarhound we know that he has a long, heavy head with a flat skull and a pointed muzzle, a broad chest and back, long legs with heavy bones and raised loins; the body was somewhat taller and longer than that of the more compact bull-baiter (see the first series of drawings, page 15). The Molossus was large, powerfully built and long-coated. This breed, which included animals of sheepdog types as well as mountain dogs, was also used for hunting. This sets clear limits to size and weight because the latter, if excessive, have an adverse effect on the endurance which is needed for hunting.

From the work by Phébus it appears that dogs of the heavy mastiff type such as the Bordeaux dog of his period (around 1350) were considerably lighter, more sinewy and nimbler than the present representatives of this breed. Practically all the descendants of the old working breeds differ considerably in regard to size from the original working dogs. In earlier times the requirements imposed on the behavior and external form of a dog were determined by work. Further limitations were imposed by his environment.

The Alano, the Spanish bull-baiter, did not resemble the bulldog or Boxer breeds but was instead light and long-legged.

The Doberman is now, as far as his external appearance is concerned, the opposite in many respects of the Rottweiler. Yet the direct ancestor of this dog - the Landpinscher (Boerenpinscher) as

Hauck calls him - was of a coarser and sturdier type. He had a rounder rib cage than his descendant, much less refinement and a less well defined head.

The Rottweiler and the Landpinscher are related, and the Rottweiler was used along with the Manchester Terrier to create the Doberman. The close relationship between the original Rottweiler and the first Dobermans and the great external agreement between them led to selective breeding in which the differences were accentuated.

The following is a quotation freely translated from Rudolf Löns:

"Driving a few head of cattle, especially a nervous and refractory calf, is one of the most difficult tasks that a dog can perform as it requires a great deal of strength, agility and endurance. The dog must be strong enough to call to order the heaviest steer with a bite in the knee; he must be quick enough to get hold of it from behind without being kicked and must have sufficient endurance to keep going day after day, continually running to and fro, trotting and galloping, leaping and barking.

This hard, tiring and noisy work calls for a serene temperament which knows how to distinguish between clumsiness, fear and malice, which is not put off by any distraction, and which can conserve its strength and make full use of its capacity. In the cattle dog sensitivity and patience must be combined with inexorable severity; the cattle must not be afraid of him because this will make the herd wild and difficult to control, but they must recognize his superiority and respect it.

Towards his master the cattle dog must be docile and willing, and must pay attention to the slightest signal; towards the rest of the world he must be hostile, distrustful and ready to assist at any time. The sense organs are all employed to an equal degree with no special emphasis on any one of them; the ear must pay attention to the sounds of the herd and the master's voice, the eye must at the same time observe every movement of the cattle, the master's actions and the surroundings, and the nose must be capable of following the trail of an escaped animal and that of the master.

The work of the cattle dog takes place chiefly under the open sky in fields and on roads. At home he can be used as a farm watch dog or as a draught animal. Farm dog and cattle dog alike are clothed not in thick fur, but in the short rough coat of the long-distance runner who needs no warm covering. The eyes, peering continually in all directions and troubled all the time by sunlight and dust, are set obliquely and rather narrow; the gaze is restless, the eyes move continually to and fro, the expression is watchful. The nose is medium sized and broad. The cattle dog is rather heavily built, cleanly proportioned, muscular and with heavy bones. The trunk is broad, with a deep but not very roomy chest, compact and therefore maneuverable. The angulation of the hindquarters is steep, giving endurance at the cost of speed. The gait comprises the short and characteristically swinging amble, the rapid trot covering a great deal of ground and the short and powerful gallop. The neck is of medium length and very strong, the skull broad and heavy, the muzzle medium to long, the mouth large and the teeth strong. The tail is bristly, short to medium in length and generally carried low.

In North and Central Germany a butcher's dog predominates which has an extended build, a long trunk, a long shoulder and a long upper front leg which forms an angle of 90 degrees with the shoulder, the hindquarters are of corresponding shape and angulation. The head is long, the skull very broad, the muzzle long. The color is predominantly black with dark brown and white markings; grey with light brown also occurs.

In South Germany the cattle dog is shorter and more compact. There is no difference in character between the two types".

Whether the working performance described in this passage can be expected of the present Rottweiler is open to doubt. He has become too big and less maneuverable and agile, and his liveliness and speed of reaction are less. His short compact muzzle is a handicap when nipping cows in the hocks; he bites too hard, his body approaches several centimeters closer to that of the cow which can make the difference between receiving and avoiding a kick if the cow steps backwards, and he bites too high (because of his size) which reduces the value of beef cattle.

His considerably larger head is a disadvantage when traveling long distances; because of the extra weight a large-headed Rottweiler, after trotting for about an hour, carries his head noticeably lower than another of the same breed with a lighter skull. The result of this is more dust in the eyes and an inferior angle of vision. The dog is aware of the ground close by but sees little of what is happening at a distance. The inability of the present Rottweiler to amble is also a drawback. The ambling gait has a very specific function for the cattle dog which can use it to attain easlily every speed up to 9.3 miles per hour and, if necessary, break readily into a gallop. As speed increases, dogs that cannot amble have to make the difficult and tiring transition from walking to trotting. The variation in tempo is not continuous; either they walk at up to 2.48 miles per hour or else they trot at 3.73 miles per hour or more. They are not capable of going at the intervening speed of 3.1 miles per hour. For a dog that must continually change direction and speed, the amble is extremely practical. The efficiency of the action is increased, and there is no waste of energy. For traveling a long distance at the same speed the ratio of energy consumed to ground covered is less in the case of the amble than in the trot. Excess of size in the working cattle dog has advantages for trotting and ambling but disadvantages for galloping. A marked disadvantage of ambling is the heavy wear and tear on the spinal vertebrae. People were therefore justified in wanting to breed out this hereditary trait, but the attempt has not been completely successful; we still see Rottweilers with a preference for ambling.

If we compare the present Rottweiler with the dogs of around

1910, we see that a great many color types have disappeared. The shoulder height has increased; this is best seen from photographs. The fact is underlined by measurements taken of 5 Rottweilers (2 dogs and 3 bitches) which served with the Austrian army in the first World War.

The three bitches had shoulder heights of 21 5/8, 21 15/16 and 21 7/16 inches respectively, and the two dogs 23 1/8 and 24 5/8 inches. The body lengths were 22 1/16, 22 1/2, 24 13/16, 24 and 26 inches. The figures are reproduced in the following table:

	Nelly ♀	Hella ♀	Greta ♀	Rolf ♂	Sherlock ♂
Height	21 5/8	21 15/16	21 7/16	23 1/8	24 5/8
Length of trunk	22 1/16	22 1/2	24 13/16	24	26
Width of chest	5 1/8	4 13/16	5 1/8	5 11/16	5 1/8
Depth of chest	6 15/16	7 1/16	8 3/16	8 3/8	9 5/8
Width of counter (From point of shoulder to point of shoulder)				6 11/16	
Circumference of chest	21 5/8	21 1/4	22 3/4	24 3/8	26
Length of head	8 7/16	7 3/4	8 9/16	8 3/4	9 1/4
Width of zy-gomatic arch	4 5/8	4 1/2	4 5/8	4 13/16	5 3/8
Depth of muzzle	2 15/16	2 13/16	2 15/16	3 1/4	3 3/8
Circumference of skull	15 3/8	14 15/16	16 1/8	16 3/4	17 5/16
Width of hips	4 3/16	4 1/2	4 13/16	4 13/16	5 1/8
Weight	44.09	48.50	57.31	54.01	61.72

NOTE: All measurements in inches and weight in pounds.

This shows that the Rottweiler of today is larger, much longer and somewhat heavier and has acquired a much larger and more mastiff-like head. The dog that had the blood of hunting dogs as well as of mastiff-like ancestors and whose appearance displayed Pinscher-like features has become a typical Mastiff. The latter is a dog whose head is characterized by an extremely wide zygomatic arch, a round skull with pronounced stop and a cranium which noticeably predominates over the muzzle. This compressed head is historically inappropriate for the Rottweiler, and also has real disadvantages. The windpipe associated with it is often narrower, sometimes conspicuously so, and the mucuous membrane is noticeably smaller. To take in the same quantity of air the dog has to breathe more rapidly and with greater effort. According to Hauck, dogs with shortened heads have a more limited life span, probably because of the constant difficulty of breathing. The short muzzle is right for fighting dogs; it confers the ability to bite hard, hold fast and inflict severe wounds, but it is not appropriate for a cattle dog.

The shorter muzzle has the disadvantage that it is more difficult to grasp and hold on to large objects. The shorter the jaw, the wider the mouth must be opened to enclose an object and the closer the object is to the tongue which in turn compresses the throat, thus making it more difficult to breathe and to perspire when the temperature is high.

The muzzle of normal length (half or a little over half the total length of the skull) is the most efficient for a working dog.

Furthermore a compressed head with a round skull brings with it a round and somewhat protruding eye and loose skin on the head. Despite this, the breed standard calls for an almond-shaped eye with close-fitting eyelids and no dewlaps. These two things are in conflict with each other. The almond-shaped eye is much less troubled by sunlight and dust and with tight skin there is less risk of entropion and ectropion (hereditary defects of the eyelids). Moreover the short muzzle stimulates inadequately developed dentition.

As long ago as 1930 Hauck warned against exaggerating the type of head, specialist judge and ADRK Chief Breed Warden (an official with great authority in the sphere of breeding) did the same in 1963. Hauck stressed the importance of assessing the ratio of skull to muzzle, in view of the large number of dogs with heavy, broad, over-developed skulls and comparatively short muzzles.

Unfortunately he had few successors and he himself soon disappeared from the scene. The skull has since continued to become more Mastiff-like. In selection for breeding and judging at shows there is an attempt to bring about a progressive 'improvement' of the type of head. We shall not have long to wait for an alteration of the breed standard on this point. Hauck remarked once that those who are called upon to assume responsibility for a breed not infrequently make the mistake of wanting to define the type of head too rigorously. Never were truer words spoken.

In the pedigreed dog there are four different types of bite: the pincer bite, the scissor bite, overshot and undershot. The Rottweiler standard, like most others, calls for a scissor bite. This is an unbiological demand. The pincer bite is normal in all wild canids, and should also be so for the pedigreed dog. In requiring a scissor bite in the dog, one imposes a norm borrowed from the human bite, and asks for something which is not applicable to the dog. In chewing movements the dog keeps his upper jaw still and only moves his lower jaw. Man can move his jaws up and down, sideways and left and right, forwards and backwards. The dog can only make an up and down movement. His much tougher food - meat and bones - requires a firm support for the limited jaw movement of which he is capable.

The large canine teeth and molars also render horizontal grinding movements impossible.

Not only all wild dogs - wolves, coyotes, jackals, etc. - but also all predatory animals without exception have a pincer bite. The scissor bite is for them an abnormal and unnatural phenonmenon. Man uses his incisors to bite off pieces of food; the dog does this with his molars. The incisors are used in grooming and searching for fleas, in gnawing off the last remains of skin and meat from bones, in removing the membrane from newborn puppies, etc. The pincer bite is much more efficient for these purposes than the scissor bite. The idea that with the pincer bite the incisors and the canine teeth wear more quickly is generally speaking incorrect. The extent to which the mouth is closed, giving rise to wear, depends not on the incisors but on the molars.

In prehistory there were representatives of the dog family which managed perfectly well with a short muzzle, a compressed skull and a pincer bite. The longer muzzle had advantages which led to an evolution in that direction. Trumler not only describes it as the height of stupidity to speak of a healthy pincer bite as a fault, but also expresses the view that the scissor bite is a symptom of a degenerative phenomenon which occurs all too often in domestic animals, namely the shortening of the lower jaw (see also Chapter 5).

Absence of premolars is however not a recent phenomenon; it is observed also in dog skulls in Inca burials and in mummified Egyptian dogs. The lack of a single premolar does not reduce the efficiency of the bite, and to penalize it in pedigreed dogs by prohibiting their use for breeding is going too far.

The standard speaks of 'good' articulation and describes this rather precisely. Whether it really is good is the question; the highest endurance is achieved with somewhat steeper articulation.

The landing after a jump is also better supported by forequarters which are not so well articulated. The ideal Rottweiler is supposed to be 'cat-footed'; it is wrong to require an active predator like the dog to have the relatively small foot of a climber like the cat.

The standard speaks of a broad, deep chest; this too is not a natural characteristic of active predators. The latter have fairly narrow chests which give more speed and a better operation of the propulsive mechanism. The broad chest gives stability when standing, which is practical for cattle, for example, which graze for long periods.

The French stance is named as a working fault, and also loose feet. There is no justification for these statements either; all wolves show these 'working faults', and the efficiency of their physical build requires no demonstration.

Compared with the domestic dog the wolf has elbows which are more turned in towards the body, giving greater firmness. In the Rottweiler the broad chest necessitates a looser attachment of the shoulder in order to avoid walking with front legs very wide apart (tiring and not efficient). The deep chest and relatively short paws strengthen this tendency towards loose shoulders, and lack of firmness in the shoulder causes the early look of weakness in the chest.

The standard calls for the Rottweiler to have coarse, heavy bones. It must be recognized that these are not as hard and robust as somewhat finer bone material, and that they are more subject to inherited cartilage defects and rickets. The experts are amazed that wild members of the dog family are able to survive despite faults which are supposed to be 'harmful to health' and which would lead at shows to their being described as 'badly built'. Perhaps it is the way external appearance is viewed at shows that is at fault.

Particular attention must be paid to endurance and gait, says the standard. There is little scope for this in the limited time and space available in the show ring. For this reason, and because of frequent breeding with beauty champions, the Rottweiler has lost much of his 'almost inexhaustible endurance'. Yet it is important to investigate thoroughly the capacity of the dog in this respect. This is illustrated by an incident during a German show held on a hot day when the Federal Champion *Ferro von der Löwenau,* regarded as 'valuable for breeding', collapsed panting and died the same evening.

The conclusion of what has been said above is that there is no need to despair if one is told at a show that one's dog is badly articulated, has loose feet, has the French stance at the front and is somewhat cow-hocked behind, has a narrow and shallow chest and that the bones could be heavier. Such a dog shows more of the picture of the true working dogs and their wild forebears than do the beauty champions. We do not need to let all dog breeds disappear or try fanatically to recreate the Rottweler as he was in grandmother's day, but we would do well to find the way back to somewhat more natural forms in the Rottweiler, subordinate external appearance to efficiency and the highest standard of health, and interpret the points of the breed in a broad and flexible way as far as appearance is concerned.

4. On feeding and exercise

Good feeding is very important for the attainment of the physical condition called health. This is equally true for people as well as for dogs. Dogs can be fed on household scraps, on proprietary foods or on a special diet of one's own preparation.

The feeding schedule given below is the third category and, although it involves a good deal of work, it provides in my opinion the best possible diet for a dog. The schedule is derived in the main from the ideas of Juliette de Baïracli-Levy ('My Dog in Sickness and Health' in *'Healthy Puppies'*) and has been tried out on my own Rottweilers. The latter have always been particularly healthy and have remained free of hip dysplasia.

Feeding from birth to four weeks

Up to four weeks, bitch's milk (real or synthetic) is given exclusively. As the puppy's gastric juices contain little hydrochloric acid, solid food and especially meat are incompletely digested. This leads to the formation of too much acid and favorable conditions for the development of worms and ailments.

It is astonishing that some breeders give meat to puppies which are barely two weeks old, although nature indicates quite clearly when weaning should begin.

a. The female wolf starts to regurgitate predigested food when her pups are about four weeks old. The dog is certainly very different from the wolf, but we should not assume that its digestive organs have undergone changes. This also applies to the dog as to the earliest time for taking food other than bitch's milk.

b. Puppies get their first incisors when they are about 3-4 weeks old, the eye teeth in the fourth week, and the molars in the fifth and sixth weeks. The milk teeth are fully developed at the age of 8 weeks. This too shows that the dog is not equipped to take anything but liquid food before the fourth week. The development of the milk teeth shows when weaning should begin and when it can be completed.

c.   Puppy feces change color around the fourth week, even when the diet remains the same; from mustard colored to dark brown. This is a sign of the change in the digestion which indicates that a change in the menu must take place.

The less easily digestible protein-rich foods must be given in the correct quantity and from the correct age. If one gives too much or begins too soon, the risk of kidney trouble is increased.

Weaning
Weaning is begun by giving the puppies a meal of milk and honey from the 28th day at 12 Noon and 4 P.M.

Feeding between the fourth and fifth weeks
When the puppies are almost 4 1/2 weeks old their menu is as follows:

8 A.M.	- Milk with honey
12 Noon	- Some barley flakes, soaked for 12 hours in milk
4 P.M.	- as at 8 A.M.
8 P.M.	- as at 12 Noon

Feeding after the fifth week

8 A.M.   - milk with honey

12 Noon   - corn flakes, soaked for 12 hours in milk, plus addition I which consists (per dog) of: some chopped raisins, one teaspoonful of chopped margarine, one teaspoonful of Gestaal*, one teaspoonful of wheat germ and some finely grated fruit (apple, etc.) followed by some old whole-meal bread.

Gestaal = barley

4 P.M.   - 25 grams of meat cut up and sprinkled with one teas-
             poonful of bran and one teaspoonful of bone meal.

8 P.M.   - 25 grams of meat cut up with addition II which con-
             sists of: one dessertspoonful of liver oil (when there is
             an 'R' in the month) or olive oil (in the summer
             months), one teaspoonful of powdered seaweed, one
             dessertspoonful of raw, very finely chopped green
             vegetables (parsley or celery, peppermint, watercress,
             dandelion leaves and tops, etc.), one teaspoonful of
             bone meal.

These quantities are gradually increased.

Feeding after the eighth week

8 A.M.   - milk with honey (1/7 liter)

12 Noon   - 30 grams of soaked corn flakes plus addition I. The
             quantities of Gestaal and wheat germ are doubled.
             One slice of old whole-meal bread.

4 P.M.   - 100 grams of meat (cut up in 1 cm. pieces) with 1
             teaspoonful of bran and 2 teaspoonsful of bone
             meal.

8 P.M.   - 100 grams of meat (cut up in 1 cm. pieces) plus addi-
             tion II. The quantity of greens is increased to 1½
             dessertspoonsful and the quantity of bone meal is 2
             teaspoonsful.

These quantities are gradually increased.

Feeding after the sixteenth week

8 A.M.   - discontinue

12 Noon   - 80 grams of soaked corn flakes plus addition I, con-
             sisting of: some chopped raisins, one tesponful of
             chopped margarine, one tablespoonful of Gestaal,

one tablespoonful of wheat germ, grated fruit. Followed by two slices of old whole-meal bread.

4 P.M.   - 300 grams of meat, sprinkled with some bran and two teaspoonsful of bone meal.

8 P.M.   - 300 grams of meat, 1½ tablespoonsful of liver oil or olive oil (in summer), 1½ teaspoonsful of powdered seaweed, 2 tablespoonsful of raw, very finely chopped green vegetables, 2 teaspoonsful of very finely chopped garlic or onion, 2 teaspoonsful of bone meal.

These quantities are gradually increased.

Feeding after the seventh month

12 Noon   - 120 grams of soaked corn flakes plus addition I (see sixteenth week), plus three slices of old whole-meal bread.

4 P.M.   - discontinue

6 P.M.   - 1¼ kg. of meat, 1½ tablespoonsful of bone meal, bran, 1½ teaspoonsful of powdered seaweed, 2 dessertspoonsful of green vegetables, now and then some grated root vegetables or raw beetroot, 2 teaspoonsful of chopped garlic or onion.

Feeding after the twelfth month

12 Noon   - 180 grams of soaked corn flakes, with additions as described at seventh month.

6 P.M.   - 1½ kg. of meat, with additions as described at seventh month.

Remarks on the various foodstuffs.

Milk: preferably completely raw (not pasteurized or heat-treated), always at body temperature, not boiled and never straight from the refrigerator. Milk is never given in excessive amounts and always mixed with honey or corn flakes, as it will otherwise curdle in the dog's stomach.

Honey: one teaspoonful of honey is added to each cupful of milk. Honey is much better than sugar (also much used in feeding dogs) and besides sucrose, fructose and glucose, contains oils, dextrine, albumin, waxy materials, fats, malic acid, formic acid and enzymes.

Cereals: the relevant varieties are oats, barley, wheat and rye. The first two should not be cooked. If they are in the form of flakes, they must be soaked overnight in milk (at the beginning of weaning) or in vegetable water. Wheat and rye are best ground and lightly cooked to make them digestible for the dog. In the case of puppies, 2/3 of the cereal food consists of barley flakes which are very easily digested, and 1/3 of oat flakes or lightly cooked rye meal. Rye contains much vitamin E and fluorine in a natural form. Instead of preparing one's own cereal mixture, one can use the so-called 'Health Flakes' made by Beaphar (Raalte) in accordance with De Baïracli-Levy's recipe.

Meat: always give raw. The higher the quality of the meat, the more easily digestible it is - important in weaning. Only 'red' meat (not pigmeat) is given before the fifth month. After that it can be replaced in part by raw offal (tripe and stomachs, unwashed if possible). To provide all the necessary amino acids, different complementary proteins should be mixed together (variation in the meat diet). Meat and cereals are never given together as the latter provide a much smaller stimulus for the secretion of hydrochloric acid in the gastric juices. Bacteria in the meat are only killed if the hydrochloric acid concentration is not too low. When meat and cereals are eaten together, the secretion of hydrochloric acid is less and the disinfecting operation of the gastric juices is inadequate. This leads in addition to incomplete digestion of the meat, lactic fermentation and formation of gas. The acid reaction in the stomach is too little for digesting meat and too much for digesting cereals, which are also not satisfactorily digested as a result.

Bran may, however, be given with meat and forms an exception to the rule.

Fats: a dog can take a lot of fat and needs a good deal of it. Hence, there is no sense in supplying lean meat. It should be borne in mind, however, that all fats go bad quickly and are then extremely harmful to health.

Wheat germ and Gestaal: both of these can, like bran, be obtained in the so-called health food shop. Among other things they contain - as do yeast flakes - the vitamin of the B group, if only to a limited extent. In order to moderate somewhat your dog's rate of growth, no yeast flakes are given before the age of 12 months. After the first year we alternate wheat germ, Gestaal and yeast flakes. Gestaal contains a lot of phosphorus and can cause miscarriage and stillbirths.

Eggs: a raw egg is given on alternate days with the meat meal from about the tenth week. The fact that raw eggs contain a material which destroys vitamin B is not a reason for boiling the egg.

Bones: after the last meat meal, we give the dog an uncooked bone. Among other things this stimulates a solid motion and consequent pressing out of the anal gland. On days when a bone is given the quantity of bone meal is halved.

From the age of 4 months dogs eat nothing up to 12 Noon. From the seventh month the dog has a half-day fast once a week; the 12 Noon meal is put off to 6 P.M. and the 6 P.M. meal is omitted. From the age of 24 months the dog fasts for a whole day once a week, followed by a meatless day (two cereal meals).

Fasting gives the stomach a rest and promotes health. Tests have shown that animals live much longer when they eat 10 per cent less than they are supposed to according to the book. The quantity of meat for the adult dog must be closely adjusted to the amount of exercise that he gets. More meat than necessary leads to overloading of the kidneys. Once the dog is fully grown, the quantity of protein in his food is somewhat reduced, and a further reduction takes place after he is six years old.

A growing Rottweiler should consume the equivalent of one twentieth of his body weight each day; three-quarters of this should consist of food of animal origin.

If the feeding dish is not completely cleared at once, the quantity of cereal and meat is reduced by a fifth for several days. After that the usual quantity can be given once again. Great care should be taken to ensure that the dog does not get too fat; it should be possible to feel the ribs, and the loin should be clearly narrower than the rib cage.

The measurements of a fully grown Rottweiler weighing 45 kg. in terms of calories, protein, fat and carbohydrates are as follows (according to Descambre):

		Protein	Fat	Carbohydrates
at rest	2226 cal.	76 g	20 g	420 g
light work	2567 cal.	98 g*	24 g	476 g
medium work	2950 cal.	126 g	28 g	532 g
heavy work	3709 cal.	140 g	35 g	700 g

* = 98 g protein = 490 g muscle meat = 735 g offal (tripe)

Green vegetables: dogs need greens but cannot digest the cellulose in the cell walls. Wild dogs eat the half-digested stomach contents of their prey, but for domestic dogs the greens must be lightly cooked or (which is much better) very finely chopped.

Plants contain an average of 40 different chemical constituents, and at flowering times the number increases to 100. Most of these materials have not been scientifically investigated, but it is clear that they contribute to the health of the dog.

There is no need for large quantities, but here too some variation is desirable.

Hip dysplasia (HD) and feeding in the growing period
The rate of growth is determined by the dog's metabolism, by the

intake of calories in relation to the energy consumption, and above all by the quantity of vitamin B_2 in the diet.

Fast growing dogs are more likely to get HD than those that grow slowly. HD is unknown in Greyhounds; dogs of this breed develop physically at a much slower tempo than the Rottweiler. Poorly developed musculature of the hindquarters (especially the muscles in the hip) and a large heavy body also lead to the emergence of HD. The bigger and heavier a dog is at 8 months, the greater the risk of dysplastic hip joints. An experiment with German Mastiffs from dysplastic parents shows how over-feeding led to lethargy, enormous body growth, the development of a heavy skeleton and pronounced hip dysplasia. The period in which over-feeding and accelerated growth are most harmful lies between 3 and 8 months. The quantities of calcium and phosphorus in the dog's food are very important. Both must be given in adequate quantities and in the correct proportion. Even when the proportion is right, too much is as harmful as too little.

The proportions which the various foodstuffs should occupy in the total diet are dependent on the size of the dog. Smaller dogs need relatively more vitamins; they require a high-grade diet while large dogs need more food that is not so high-grade.

The so-called complete dry foods make no allowance for this; they are intended for all kinds of dogs and will be compounded in such a way as to prevent vitamin deficiencies in the most demanding users. Dogs of large breeds which daily eat the large quantities of these dry foods appropriate to their size take in larger quantities of vitamins than they need. This is harmful in the growing period. The larger quantity of vitamin B_2 leads to accelerated development. Dry foods are, therefore, less good for dogs of large breeds than for those of small ones. Anyone who wants to feed his Rottweiler on these will do best to wait until the dog is a year old. There is the further question of whether an artificially compounded, colored and preserved food contains all that a living organism needs. Interested parties (and others) will assure you that it does, but I am not convinced by their arguments.

It is important for a puppy to have frequent contact with young children.

Edda vom Ingenhof with her two-day old puppies.

A good Rottweiler - friendly, quiet, steady and a great friend of children: *Moritz vom Silahopp* (Brutus von der Kurmark x Queen von der Solitude).

A demonstration with Rottweilers trained in Holland as guard dogs.

The Dutch Rottweiler Club's behavior test: sub-section 6, the slowly closing circle.

The German Rottweiler Club's test of value for breeding; *Ari vom Waldhuck* attacks the running 'criminal'.

Encounters with other animals can form a part of the enriched environment. The young dog has assumed a cautious attitude in response to the lunges of the cock.

Pecking order relationships evolve through play-fighting.

The time is not long past when it was thought that a complete diet could be made up of proteins, fats and carbohydrates. It was not until later that vitamins, mineral salts, the different varieties of protein, saturated and unsaturated fatty acids, trace elements, enzymes, etc. were discovered. Because dry foods only contain the materials which have so far been identified, a package of natural foodstuffs is to be preferred. Moreover, making up one's own food packages provides the opportunity of separating proteins and carbohydrates in the interest of digestibility. Natural foodstuffs have a balanced composition; this is important because it is not only the 'active' materials that have a function - the accompanying or neutral materials also contribute to the effect. For this reason also synthetic vitamins do not operate in quite the same way as vitamins in their natural form.

Excercise

A young dog needs to be taken for walks a good deal, especially on natural terrain such as sand or grass, so long as he enjoys it, does not have a full stomach, and does not go lame or show symptoms of fatigue.

Dogs that get a lot of exercise grow in a more balanced way and probably grow rather less. Balanced growth promotes the development of good joints. Through frequent exercise the muscle mass of the hindquarters becomes stronger and the head of the thigh bone is pressed well into the hip socket. Here too the saying applies that 'the function forms the organ'. A much used joint becomes a good joint.

I have taken all my young Rottweilers from the age of 10 weeks for 8-10 kilometer walks every day at an easy pace. These dogs developed great endurance and sound joints. One of them, at only 20 months enjoyed running for 38 kilometers alongside a bicycle (off lead, at an easy pace and with an interval for rest).

Every healthy Rottweiler pup - provided he is not too fat - is capable of taking long walks. Inability to do so indicates poor physique. If a Rottweiler of 5 months is fully trained and not obese, he can be taken for short distances with a bicycle. He should be off the lead so that he can determine his own speed; his master does not cycle faster than 7-8 km per hour. When the dog is more than a year old there is a daily cycle trip of 15 km at a speed of almost 13 km per hour to work off surplus energy.

Suggestions that taking a dog out too soon with a bicycle is bad for him are not based on practical experience or on the results of scientific investigation.

After cycling for such a distance one dismounts about 1½ km from home and completes the journey at a walking pace. The dog does not get the chance to cool off on a cold surface. Stone and concrete are not suitable for a dog to lie on (nor as a kennel floor); this increases the risk of kidney, bladder, intestinal and prostate infections. A run should, therefore, be laid on grass or sand or have a floor of wooden planks.

Prolonged exercise results in strong circulation of blood through the muscles, capillaries and ligaments, and the widening of the vascular tissues. If sudden cooling occurs, the muscle cells contract too rapidly and there is a slackening in the removal of metabolic products (including lactic acid). The result is the muscle proteins absorbing a great deal of fluid and in muscle hardening which has an adverse effect on the functioning of the muscles.

5. Responsible breeding

Animals that live in a natural environment are constantly subject to a many-sided process of selection. This applies to all aspects of the animal and of its functioning except the one which is most highly valued by dog breeders - beauty of appearance. The criterion in natural selection is that of efficiency in the sense of the best possible adaptation to the demands of the environment. This efficiency is concerned with behavior, physiques, the manner of locomotion, the operation of senses and organs, etc.

The surroundings in which breed dogs move impose quite different demands. As a result such dogs have largely become cultured artifacts which could hardly survive in a natural environment. If the dog is not to become a barely viable creation which is totally dependent on man, reproducing itself with the help of hormone injections and artificial insemination, bringing puppies into the world by caesarian delivery and having them fed with artificial milk, it is necessary in breeding dogs to allow faults of natural selection to play a part.

Domestication implies a one-sided specializaton with the loss of qualities which enabled the wild animal to excel, but not the loss of all the qualities of the wild animal and the growth of creatures totally dependent on man.

The aim of dog breeding should be the production of animals which are in the first place dogs, and only in the second place, breed dogs.

To achieve this, animals should meet the following (partly overlapping) requirements:

a. Constant good health and high resistance to disease;

b. a good physical constitution and the ability to do well on a plain diet;

c. strong stamina, good locomotive apparatus which is efficient and not subject to premature wear and tear (arthritis) and well functioning organs and senses;

d. appropriate behavior: cheerful, balanced, unafraid, showing intelligence, peaceable and tolerant towards people and other dogs;

e. Possession of a good deal of the 'package of instincts' of the wild dog, so that among other things mating and whelping can take place practically without human intervention;

f. no serious inherited defects in the genetic endowment;

g. fertility and the ability to produce healthy offspring.

To achieve (b) above, it is sufficient for animals to show a certain measure of conformity in their external appearance with the standard of their breed. In the practice of breeding, attention is paid almost exclusively to the latter. Many people think that 'improving the breed' means producing dogs which will be marked 'excellent' at shows. It is a misconception to think that a 'beautiful' dog (beautiful in the sense of conforming to the standard, which often makes unnaturalness the norm and abnormality the rule) is a desirable thing to have. Breed dogs are mainly bred and owned on account of the pleasure which they give to their owners in social intercourse. This pleasure diminishes considerably and can even change to distress if one sees one's dog continually suffering or sickening when a long walk or a violent leap while playing leads to lameness and pain, when the dog shows timid, panicky or highly aggressive behavior; in short, when the dog cannot function as a member of a household without causing problems.

The aim of dog breeding should be to produce animals which spare themselves and their owners all these difficulties. Dogs should be companions, not ornaments. The dog is the only domestic animal which truly lives with man; all the rest only live alongside him.

Hereditary defects can be classified as follows:

a. hereditary diseases which give rise to a more or less severe disturbance of the general wellbeing;

b. hereditary shortcomings which have a certain influence on health or performance;

c. departures from the breed standard which do not affect health or performance but represent a deviation from the prescribed goal.

The prevalence of hereditary diseases and shortcomings has increased greatly in specific populations of breed dogs. Mostly this concerns not just one, but several physical or mental defects. To get a picture of this, breed societies should make it their business to gather information. For example, an inquiry can be held for the purpose of listing the weak points of a breed: what diseases occur frequently, what are the causes of death, what are the reasons for the death of puppies (post mortem at the society's expense). After the data have been processed and analyzed priorities must be established: which defects are the most serious?

In this connection compromises will be necessary and in many cases the lesser of two evils will have to be chosen.

It is clear that faults in relation to the breed standard will have to take a very low place in the list of priorities. No sensible person will regard white chest markings or long hair in the Rottweiler as a serious fault merely because the standard happens to consider these noticeable external features undesirable. A strong over-bite should certainly come high on such a list because it is often associated with all kinds of other abnormalities in the head, and sometimes even with epilepsy; a strong under-bite can stand low in the list because it causes no harm to health or well-being, as witness the fact that there are plenty of sound and vigorous Boxers. It is self-evident that dogs with really serious hereditary diseases must not be used for breeding, as well as - and this people find rather less self-evident - both their parents and their litter brothers and sisters. Inbreeding must be practiced in order to select good young male dogs.

With a good gene pool and correct selection, inbreeding and line breeding present no danger. With the avoidance of inbreeding and line breeding, a bad tendency remains only temporarily concealed. A few cases of close line breeding in the Rottweiler over the last few years gave results which were not encouraging.

Genetic degeneration usually shows itself more in the male than in the female descendants. Whenever in a breed or line, the number of bitches in the progeny is noticeably larger than the number of dogs, this can be an indication that something is amiss. In this connection it is important to find out in what period of year the puppies were born, because there are more bitches in litters born after or at the end of the summer. In warm periods, and especially in heat waves, there is a drop in the fertility of female animals and the survival chances of fertilized egg cells. The egg cells from which bitches will develop are more resistant as a rule to higher temperatures.

Correct selection in breeding dogs of a working breed is not possible without the application of an endurance test. Before a dog like the Rottweiler is allowed to be bred from, he should be subjected once in every two year period to a long distance walk of 30-35 kilometers. With dogs that can complete the course without problems, it can be assumed that their locomotion apparatus and a number of important organs are functioning satisfactorily. If one wants to get an impression of the performance capability of a dog in this area, training programs can be carried out at the same time with intervals for rest in which the time is measured to the moment when the dog stops panting and shows willingness to be on the move again.

Responsible breeding of animals does not depend solely on choosing the right objectives. An adequate degree of knowledge is also necessary to be able to select and combine meaningfully. By far the largest number of abnormalities are caused by hereditary mechanisms which are much more complicated than the laws of Mendel. The knowledge of dog breeders has failed to keep pace with the progress of genetics; many have gone no further than Mendel or have not even proceeded as far as studying his laws. It is a pity that practically all the findings of modern genetics (extrachromosomal inheritance, behavioral genetics, population genetics) are not known in the dog world. Dog breeders are often not disposed to accept the genetic consequences of an abnormality if these cannot be accounted for in accordance with Mendelian laws. This is a major error since with a particular type of heredity the inherited factor can only be demonstrated by statistical methods.

Breeders must know what is meant by concepts such as the coefficient of inbreeding (the criterion for the increase of homozygosis) and the degree of relatedness, which factors determine the bases of breeding, and what is meant by the method of 'controlled heterosis'. They must also be fully aware that in a responsible progeny investigation a dog must be mated with at least six bitches which have been sired by at least three different dogs. These dogs must not be full brothers, but at most half-brothers.

At least 35 puppies must be tested. If the progeny investigation is concerned with behavior and hip dysplasia, a Rottweiler will be very suitable for breeding if 85 per cent of the puppies pass a behavior test and 75 per cent have normal hip joints.

Anyone who breeds a litter now and again with one or two bitches can do little more than mate two healthy, lively animals which have passed a behavior test, function well in a family, do not bite little children and have never gone lame. Such a breeder, too, must want to know that no serious inherited faults can be passed on. To get a picture of this it is necessary as a minimum to obtain reliable information about the litter brothers and sisters of both partners and of their parents. As a rule of thumb it can be assumed that all dogs from a litter are capable of passing on all the characteristics present in that litter. A dog which shows good behavior, but has five brothers and sisters who clearly do not, will transmit both his own good disposition and the bad disposition of his litter companions. Because of the numerical ratio (1 good to 5 bad) the latter will probably predominate.

Cooperation by breeders offers many more possibilities for the genuine improvement of a breed. Through joint discussion and perhaps with the help of experts, bloodlines can be established which are free of a serious hereditary fault occurring in the breed. In the most extreme case this can lead to a separate line with respect to each fault. By a series of matings two lines can be combined into a new one which is free of two faults, etc. The objective for each line must be clearly defined and one must try to achieve it by small steps.

The job of a breed society is not to stimulate attendance at shows, but to encourage responsible breeding; not to popularize the breed, but to reward sound achievements in breeding, expressed in close inbreeding without serious defects; not to further the growth of the society, but to provide for the exhange of information about the transmission of behavior characteristics and defects. No cups should be presented for beauty of appearance, but rather for excellent results in passing behavior tests and for winning working certificates. Money prizes may perhaps be awarded; money is the motive for much that is done in the dog world.

For a breed society to function in the manner described, no breeders should be allowed to sit on the governing body. Breeders and owners generally have opposite interests; the breeders wish to have as few restrictive rules as possible and to be completely free to realize their aims, whereas it benefits the owners if there are stringent breeding regulations to increase the chances of buying a good puppy. It is mainly the breeders who are aware of this antithesis and are motivated to attend meetings.

Success in fighting against hereditary defects depends on good selection and on honesty, openness and exchange of information. The latter is a problem for many breeders. Some of them would rather bite their tongue off than admit abnormalities have appeared in their kennels. Problems later with dogs from such breeders are by definition the fault of the owner. Attendance at shows is encouraged if the dog looks good, but strongly advised against if he does not conform well to the standard. Participation in a behavior test is not discouraged if it seems certain that the dog will get a good mark, but strongly discouraged if there is more uncertainty about the results.

Breeders with a sense of responsibility will help others with the object of preventing faults and failures from being repeated.

The assessment of very young puppies

With a good selection of breeding animals, behavior in the first minutes and days of life can be taken into consideration. The assessment which Trumler advises is of great value in this connection.

Trumler postulates that a dog which does not attempt within the first minutes of its life to reach the maternal breast has hereditary defects. A new-born puppy should burrow and scramble for the teat and have a good suckling reflex.

Weakness in this respect points to degeneration and loss of instinct. He gives simple guidelines for assessing behavior in this initial phase. Good puppies are those that on being freed from the membrane go at once in search of the milk source. Less good are those that at first lie still and then go searching. Worst of all are the puppies that cannot find the teat for themselves or, having found it, let it go again after they have hardly begun to drink.

If the puppy is laid on the table after being weighed, he should crawl about and move his head to and fro. If he is placed on his back, he should quickly turn over. If touched with a cold glass or metal object, he should draw back. He should crawl towards a hot water bottle of about 35°C (95°F). A puppy that lies still until he is picked up again is scarcely viable. Some bitches know when there is something wrong with a puppy; they will not allow him to drink (if indeed he does so) and/or work him out of the litter basket. It makes little sense to punish a bitch for this and take all kinds of trouble to keep such a puppy alive. A bitch that kills her own puppy because its sucking reflex is too weak behaves in a socially responsible manner and shows a sound instinct. She increases thereby the survival chances of the remaining puppies.

It is advisable, directly after the birth of puppies, to provide them with identifying marks so that they can be distinguished from each other. These marks (which may be applied with, among other things, nail varnish, aluminum paint or different colored ribbons) will make it easier to keep records. The puppies that show the desired behavior at this stage will also be the first to have their eyes and ears open, will soon show a good sense of balance and motor coordination and will, in short, be the most viable. A breeder who wants to keep a bitch for himself in order to breed further must select her in the first place on the basis of these data. Only the most viable dogs can be used successfully for breeding purposes.

In the Netherlands pedigrees are issued by the Dutch Kennel Club at Amsterdam, and breed societies are unable to lay down any compulsory requirements with which breeders must comply. Neither (with one exception) does the Kennel Club, which has therefore become a sort of administrative office.

In the Federal Republic (Germany) the situation is quite different: the German Rottweiler Club (ADRK) keeps the breed book itself and controls the issue of pedigree documents. These documents are issued only where both parents have passed the 'Zuchttauglichkeitsprüfung' (test of suitability for breeding). In addition to this test, there is also a test of value for breeding, the so-called 'Körung'. The test of suitability is a coarse sieve, while the 'Körung' is a finer one with the purpose of identifying the best of the 'suitable' dogs so that relatively greater use can be made of them for breeding.

The test of suitability is open to all Rottweilers with pedigrees which have reached the age of 18 months. The 'Körung' is open to

Rottweilers which have passed the test of suitability, have reached the age of 24 months, have won a guard dog or police dog certificate, have been marked 'Very Good' or 'Excellent' at least three times at shows, and whose hip joints have been declared HD-negative, marginally negative or slightly positive by one of the university HD committees. In both tests account is taken of appearance and gait. The following are measured: height at withers, body length, circumference of chest and depth of chest. Much attention is given to the bite, and a behavior test is applied consisting of the so-called 'man work'.

The behavior test used in the 'Körung' is considerably stiffer than the one used in assessing suitablilty for breeding. Whether the dogs that pass either test really are suitable/valuable for breeding is a question which can only be answered by examination of their progeny. Dogs can only be entered twice for the test of suitability; if they fail the behavior test in a way which leaves some hope for the future then they can have one more attempt 6 or 12 months later. Dogs can be entered four times at most for the 'Körung'; if they fail the first time (here too in the behavior test) they can try again a year later. If they pass (at the first or second attempt) they are assumed to be valuable for breeding for a period of two years. After that a (male) dog can enter again if he has sired at least three litters free of serious inherited faults, and a bitch if she has produced at least one such litter. If this is the case, and if they pass the repeated test, they count as 'angekört auf lebenszeit' (recommended for the remainder of the period allowed for breeding). It is clear that the rule with regard to the number of litters works very much to the disadvantage of the bitches which in Germany are usually allowed to whelp only once a year and in practice have a much smaller chance of satisfying the requirements. The rule about 'three litters free of serious inherited faults' for dogs is too lenient; with some perseverance it may well be possible to find a number of bitches which do not transmit the defects which the dog has in his genotype. It would be better to substitute for this requirement, a rule that under specified circumstances (minimum number of puppies, partners with a certain degree of blood relationship) no single inherited disease or shortcoming should present itself. In fact, an inbred mating should form the basis on which value for breeding is assessed.

As long as the present regulations contain no stipulation as to the number of puppies to be considered in reaching a verdict, any litter can be made to satisfy the criteria by putting down the specimens with the unwanted characteristics.

The method described above provides a certain basis of selection which is always to be preferred to the absence of any deliberate method. At the same time this system has some curious results; a dog which has eyes which are too light but which behaves particularly well is denied the title 'valuable for breeding' (even though there is clear evidence of a relationship between light eyes and intelligence in dogs); a dog with two incisors in the lower jaw which project a fraction in front of the teeth in the upper jaw might as well go home straightaway. Whatever good features he might otherwise possess, for this reason alone he cannot be declared valuable for breeding. Conversely, beautiful dogs which bite very hard are not denied or deprived of the qualification 'valuable', even if the worst hereditary defects have appeared in their progeny. Ignorance of genetics and the belief that outstanding dogs cannot transmit any faults appear to be the reason for this.

Despite these critical remarks it is still thought desirable that German dogs which have passed the 'Körung' should be used in Dutch Rottweiler breeding. Most of these dogs do a good deal of work on the training ground, and some have won the certificate Guard Dog III (SchH III) as often as thirty times. Dogs which are not well put together (particularly in the forequarter joints) do not hold out so long as a rule. Frequent performances of this work tell one nothing about physical endurance, and even less is there any certainty that these dogs will pass on their good constitutions. Rottweilers which have passed the 'Körung' early in their lives possess a considerable degree of stamina and mental hardness, but one must look out for individuals with more than average sharpness and a low threshold of irritability. Highly recommended dogs are or were *Astor vom Landgraven, Dolf vom Weiherbrünnele* and his sons, *Maik* and *Nick vom Rodenstein* who bite hard when provoked but otherwise remain quiet and steady. A drawback in choosing German Rottweilers for mating is that our eastern neighbors are even less frank about the transmission of faults than in the Netherlands.

Hereditary abnormalities

Here follows a description of a number of abnormalities which have appeared in recent years in the Dutch Rottweiler population. Both rare and less rare cases are included - the rare ones as a warning and because of their serious nature, and the less rare ones because of the possibility of encountering them. This summary has been made possible by the frankness of a number of breeders. It is probably not complete, given that in some kennels breeding takes place, though not always successfully, behind closed doors.

The enumeration may lead to the conclusion that the Rottweiler is in a worse condition than most other breeds. Nothing is further from the truth; the fact that the Rottweiler has not become a fashionable breed has spared us a great deal of misery. The same faults occur in other breeds, and other very serious ones as well. The difference lies in the fact that in Dutch Rottweiler circles there is a greater inclination to recognize one's own failures and to stimulate improvement by washing one's dirty linen in public.

Hip dysplasia (HD)

HD is an affliction which shows itself in a malformation of the hip joint. The head of the thigh bone does not fit into the socket; the head is not held firmly in the socket and can slip out and exert pressure on the edge of the socket. Both are somewhat flattened and show what might be called areas of abrasion.

The abnormality is hereditary; different pairs of genes are involved in it, and almost the only reliable method of diagnosis is by xray. As explained in the previous chapter, environmental factors play a part in its origin.

In the 1960's American researchers came to the conclusion that HD is 25 per cent hereditary and 75 per cent determined by the environment. From matings of Alsatians and Greyhounds (a breed in which HD does not occur) it appeared that the tendency to normal hip joints is dominant over the tendency to malformed joints. Two generations of mating the Alsatian-Greyhound crosses back to Alsatians produced dogs with very good hip joints.

The minor share (25 per cent) of the genotype in the origin of the abnormality tempts one to the conclusion that there is little point in selective breeding against HD. Nothing could be further from the truth; sensitivity to the environmental factors associated with the appearance of this abnormality in the Rottweiler among others is a bad sign. Good selective breeding is needed to ensure production of dogs with a high degree of environmental insensitivity in the formation of the hip joint.

In 1965 an inquiry into HD in the dog was started at the Faculty of Veterinary Science of the University of Utrecht. The inquiry was directed in particular at Rottweilers in the Netherlands. Its aim, among other things, was to demonstrate that selection against HD (exclusion of dysplastic animals) would lead to a fall in the incidences of the abnormality. It was expected that this reduction would take place slowly at first, but thereafter progressively more rapidly, until finally the abnormality would be completely eliminated.

This expectation has so far not been realized, mainly because during the course of the inquiry increasing insight into the nature of the abnormality has led to changes in the criteria. As a result of more critical assessment, many xray photographs which had earlier led to the verdict 'HD-negative' were now qualified as 'HD-slightly positive'. The fact that despite selection the number of dogs with hip joints rated as sound does not increase has given rise to much confusion.

Hip dysplasia is a defect which can cause a great deal of pain to the dog seriously affected by it. The most difficult period is around the eighth month. After the first year the pain decreases and, with a good calcium-rich diet and an appropriate amount of exercise the dog can live out its life with the complaint without further problems. In the recent past it was all too easily concluded that dysplastic dogs ought to be put down. One must always recognize that good results can be expected from systematic selection directed towards the improvement of hereditary constitution, as well as from improvement in the environmental influences.

It is clear that there is more to a dog than just its hip joints. There are no perfect dogs, and it is always necessary to make a compromise in choosing between individuals with partly desirable and partly undesirable tendencies. A dog with a bad charcter and sound hip joints is a worse companion that one with a good character and slight HD. Confirmation of HD by xray does not mean that the dog is in pain and is never an excuse for having it put down. A dog with HD can function perfectly well without being a burden to others or to itself.

Sometimes, in the case of very severe HD, the diagnosis can be made without an xray. One feels and hears the head of the thigh bone moving in and out of the sockets as the dog walks. Dogs which are more than one year old and which regularly lie on their bellies with legs stretched out in a straight line in front of and behind their bodies are always free of hip dysplasia in my experience. It does not follow that dogs which never lie in this position have hip dysplasia.

On the forms in which the results of the xray examination are reported, the following symbols and terms are used:

HD –	HD – negative
HD ∓	HD – marginally negative
HDtc	HD – slightly positive (transitional case)
HD ±	HD – slightly positive
HD +	HD – positive
HD + +	HD – positive in severe form

These definitions will probably be replaced in the near future by a system based on a scale of points which will permit greater refinement in reporting the results of the examination and make it easier for societies and breeders to draw the line between acceptability and unacceptability for breeding purposes.

As from January 1, 1972, the Dutch Kennel Club has only issued pedigrees to the progeny of Rottweilers which have been passed as free of HD by the Utrecht HD Committee (since 1976 the line has been drawn between HD tc and HD ±). This is an exceptional arrangement because usually the Kennel Club always issues pedigrees to progeny of dogs which belong to the same breed and are recorded in the breed book, even when they show serious abnormalities.

The result of this measure is that since 1972 there has been a considerable drop in the percentage of severely dysplastic dogs.
In the Federal Republic the fight against HD in the Rottweiler has been tackled in a different way. The fact that Rottweilers there are excluded from breeding for other reasons as well (behavior, working and beauty faults) has made it necessary for a gradual approach to be adopted. First of all it was forbidden to breed with severely dysplastic dogs; some time later those that were dysplastic, but not severely so, were also ruled out.

The next step will be to exclude the 'slightly positive' cases. The same point will then have been reached in a number of stages which the Dutch Rottweiler Club achieved overnight in 1971: the exclusive use of HD-negative Rottweilers for breeding. Whether this will lead in practice to the non-use of HD-tc dogs is not clear.

Little is known about the standards applied by the different universitiy HD committees. There seems every likelihood that the criteria of the Dutch (Utrecht) HD Committee are stricter than anywhere else in the world.

It is a pity that HD is almost impossile to diagnose with certainty except by the use of xrays. This is an undesirable procedure which should not take place too often. Nevertheless some dogs are exposed as much as six times to this form of radiation. They are xrayed at 7-8 months (two photographs, one with the back legs extended behind, and one with them in front),and this is repeated when they are about 18 months old (the best age for xraying a

Rottweiler). If the photographs are of unsatisfactory quality (because they are unclear, or the dog has moved), the procedure is carried out again. Some bitches with which the owner had intended to breed are sold if the xray gives little hope of completely sound hip joints. When this happens, the results of the xray are not always disclosed.

It is undesirable that the unfertilized egg cells of bitches should be exposed so often to this radiation. The question is what will be the result in the long term of xraying dogs generation after generation. There are geneticists who maintain that there is no sense at all in investigating the heredity of animals which have been in contact with xrays. Perhaps this applies only to small species such as fruit flies which are much used in studies of genetics and which are susceptible because of their small size. Perhaps it applies to all living beings, and the point is that the effect of radiation (occurrences of genetic mutations) can be observed most conveniently in small organisms.

Torn knee ligaments

Injuries to the stifle joint often cause lameness in the dog's hindquarters. These are often found to be tears in the stifle ligaments and particularly in the anterior cruciate ligament. The risk of damage arises especially from the overstretching of the joint. This can happen when the dog, while running, puts one hind foot into a hole, or misses its footing while jumping over a fence. The stifle ligament can also degenerate because of a chronic inflammation of the joint, so that a tear happens when the ligament is stretched a little too far. A torn stifle ligament results in serious lameness; a thickening of the joint capsule takes place, the mobility of the joint is reduced and an inflammation leads in most cases to chronic deformity of the joint. An operation can lead to complete recovery. In a few cases both stifles have been injured in this way, generally at different times. This problem is not uncommon among Rottweilers; the tendency to it is clearly hereditary. One Dutch beauty champion has been operated on for it, as well as his mother. The number of descendants of this dog runs into hundreds, but how many of them have been operated on or put down for this reason is not known. A relatively large number of the descendants of another Dutch dog used in Germany and also in Denmark have undergone a stifle ligament operation, including among others his grandson who was exported to Canada. In Germany it is known that *Arko vom Georgshof,* considered valuable for breeding, had the operation.

Osteochondritis dissecans (OD)

By OD is meant a disease of the joint cartilage and the bone lying beneath it. In man the trouble affects among others the shoulder, elbow and knee joints; with the dog it usually affects the shoulder. It occurs more often in dogs than in bitches, mostly appears at an age of 6-7 months and is confined to dogs of rapidly growing heavy breeds. It usually disappears at maturity.

Recent research has revealed the defect in more than 30 breeds, but of 43 cases in which OD was diagnosed in a period of two years (in a country in which the Rottweiler is more popular than the Alsatian), there were 9 Rottweilers, 6 Alsatians, 5 Dalmatians, 5 German Pointers, 4 Labradors, 3 Bernese Mountain Dogs, 2 Bobtails, 2 Irish Wolfhounds, 2 German Mastiffs, and single cases of Golden Retriever, Pyrenean Mountain, Boxer and Newfoundland.

OD results from inadequate blood supply to the cartilage and the bone during the growing period. A splinter of bone becomes detached (dissecans means 'separating') and can damage the joint and even cause a blockage. Early diagnosis of changes in the joint is possible by xray. Treatment may consist of drugs, rest and a well-balanced diet. In serious cases an operation may be one of the possibilities.

The cause of the defect is not known. OD-like changes can be evoked by administering, among other things, male and female sex hormones. Overstrain or damage to the cartilage do not appear to be able to induce the abnormality. Hormone disturbance in the growing period is dangerous, as will as overdosing with vitamins, a diet extremely rich in albumin and mineral deficiency.

A good form of exercise for dogs suffering from OD is to swim for short distances which are gradually lengthened. OD is a hereditary tendency which in the Netherlands affected, among others, the progeny of the German dogs *Arko vom Reichenbächle, LS Quick von der Solitude* and *Black von der Vohsbeckshöhe.*

Severe shortening of the lower jaw

In American Cocker Spaniels, Borzois and long-haired Dachshunds, among others, an abnormality occurs which shows itself in a shortening, and in some cases degeneration, of the lower jaw. In less serious cases this looks like a pronounced over-bite; in serious cases almost the whole of the lower jaw is missing and the dog is unable to eat normally. This abnormality can be recognized as early as three weeks after birth. It was initally assumed that the mode of inheritance was recessive and that only one pair of genes was involved. Later publications and other data make it appear that more pairs of genes play a part in the origin of the abnormality. Sex linkage does not appear. In many cases the teeth of animals with the reduced lower jaw are considerably below the normal size. If this is not a coincidence, it may constitute the prime cause of the abnormality. The jaw will not provide any more room than is necessary for the teeth; a small set of lower teeth will lead to a small lower jaw.

The number of puppies in the litters of Cocker Spaniels in which this malformation occurred was generally below average; in these litters there was a higher percentage of puppies which were stillborn, underweight or with limited capacity for survival. The inheritance pattern is very capricious and makes it difficult to convince owners of affected dogs of the need for control measures. There have been many cases of the abnormality in the Dutch Rottweiler population since 1972.

Severely shortened lower jaws were encountered, among others, in litters with descendants of the German Dogs, *Adrian vom Dämmerwald* (5 out of 10), *Dux vom Kastanienbaum* (5 out of 10) and *Arko vom Reichenbächle* (2 out of 8).

In a litter sired by a Dutch dog 8 out of 9 puppies were afflicted by the abnormality. A succeeding litter from this dog showed no signs of it, and this was seen as proof that the dog concerned had no part in the occurrence of jaw shortening. The opposite is, of course, true; both parents were 'to blame' for the abnormality in the first litter, while its absence in the second was due to the sound genotype of the bitch concerned (all the parents had a shearing bite).

A severe shortening of the lower jaw seen early in life can cease to be visible when during the shedding of teeth, the eye-teeth in the lower jaw appear before those in the upper jaw. Pressure and counter-pressure can then give rise to an apparently normal bite. If the lower jaw had been some millimeters shorter at the decisive stage, or if the eye-teeth had been in a somewhat different position, the differences of length between both jaws in the fully grown dog would have amounted to several centimeters.

Abnormalities of the larynx

The first case of a shortening of the lower jaw that came to my notice concerned a litter from a Dutch beauty champion and the German dog, *Axel vom Zimmerplatz* (a son of Bulli vom Hungerbühl). 13 puppies were born (7-6), of which 2 dogs were dead. When the eyes opened around the fourteenth day, it was seen that in five puppies the eyes were small, narrow and slanting, with a somewhat protruding conjunctival membrane. It appeared a week later that one of the puppies had a short lower jaw and was also blind, and it was put down.

When the remaining dogs were six weeks old, another male out of the original five showed a severe lack of motor coordination. He moved clumsily, had a poor sense of balance, often fell down and also gave the impression of seeing badly. Examination pointed to a brain abnormality, blindness and entropion. About the tenth week the last three puppies (out of the five) showed breathing difficulties. A malformation of the larynx was diagnosed, and one of these dogs also had poor sight. They began to eat less and, when the breathing difficulties increased and it became apparent that there was a risk of suffocation, the puppies (at about 12 weeks old) were put out of their misery.

The other puppies were healthy and vigorous and showed no sign of any abnormality. The mother of the litter had had ten puppies on two previous occasions without anything of the kind happening. The case was reported in detail to the governing bodies of the Dutch and German Rottweiler Clubs, as well as to the German club's principal breed warden (an official with very extensive powers in the field of Rottweiler breeding in Germany), but nothing happened. Breeding continued with the dog, *Axel vom Zimmerplatz* (he was an outstanding working dog), and he was even awarded the qualification 'valuable for breeding' for two years. This was taken away at the end of the period when it was found that he had a premolar missing.

An earlier litter from the bitch concerned was sired by *LS Quick von der Solitude,* who also appears in Axel's pedigree as a grandfather on the mother's side. The outcome of this mating (no abnormalities appeared) confirms the suspicion that *Axel's* paternal line has contributed a good deal to the situation described. There are unconfirmed reports that in this line (from *Bulli vom Hungerbühl)* similar troubles have occurred among the *Kanzachtal* and *Ludwigshafen See* ancestors. Some confirmation of this is given by the sight at shows of other sons of *Bulli* who, after running around the ring a few times, become very short of breath (*Malter vom Schloss Stauffenberg)* or wheeze like an old steam engine (*Axel vom Fusse der Eifel).*

As already explained, no steps were ever taken though the obvious course would have been to carry out test matings of *Bulli* with some of his daughters. *Bulli* remained 'valuable for breeding' for the rest of his life and, as European champion, club champion and Swiss champion, sired many hundreds of descendants. *Bulli's* sons were awarded high marks at shows and were much used for breeding. In a litter from a Dutch bitch with another son of *Bulli* (*Cäsar vom Fleinsbach,* a hard, tough dog which was 'therefore' regarded as valuable for breeding), nine puppies were born. Six of these were not viable and died soon after birth, while two of the others had severely shortened lower jaws. Only one puppy was normal.

There is every indication that *Bulli* was a great danger for breeding and that a number of his sons still are; not because of the inherited long coat, but rather because of the abnormalities which have been described and the sharpness and extreme irritability seen in this line. The ethologist Trumler once predicted that the canine breeds will become extinct in a short time; if there is no change in the mentality of their owners, he will certainly be proved right.

'Swimming'

By swimming in this context is meant the behavior of puppies of 3 weeks or more which cannot stand or walk and which crawl along lying flat on the ground. The first publication on this, relating to Pekingese, appeared in 1959. The condition is suspected to be hereditary. The two cases applying to the Rottweiler which have been brought into the open in the Netherlands confirm this opinion. Both concerned five puppies in a litter of eight or nine. Of the four parents, three were closely related; in one case line breeding was practiced. The unrelated animal was the German dog, *Elko vom Kastanienbaum,* who was, at the same time, the sire of another litter with a bitch also related to the other three. This litter included a dog that for a long time found it painful to rise from a lying position and had to be helped up to the age of 10 months, and another that showed reluctance to move (preferred to be carried as a puppy).

The condition can generally be remedied with careful treatment. After a considerable lapse of time it is often impossible to tell that the dogs concerned were ever affected by it. In the cases referred to here, the puppies were put down. The condition appears to be identical with the blood disease (hemophilia) in newborn dogs, caused by A-positive puppies taking up antibodies from the colostral milk of an A-negative bitch which had acquired immunity. It occurs in several different breeds; further reports are lacking in the case of the Rottweiler. One may assume that it is very rare in this breed.

The chances of 'swimmers' appearing among puppies can be reduced by using flooring material with a rough surface which provides purchase for the feet.

Entropion

Entropion is an abnormality in which the eyelid is curled inwards and the lashes irritate the eyeball. This problem occurs with, among others, Chow Chows and Rottweilers. The condition is hereditary, may be identified at 6 weeks and can be remedied by means of an operation. With many dogs which have deep-set eyes, a round head and loose skin, this abnormality can appear temporarily. A day in the hot sun (screwing up the eyes), or digging in loose sand, and by evening there is trouble. The eyes itch, the dog rubs them with its front paws, and the curling of the eyelid gets worse and worse. Massaging with the hand above and below the eyelids away from the eye can help. Precise information is not available, but it looks as though this affliction occurs less now than it once did. Statements in the literature about the mode of inheritance vary from recessive to semi-dominant.

Reproductive problems

Rottweiler dogs are not always very competent at mating. Some show little interest (especially on a warm day), other individuals do not persevere, and occasionally one does not copulate at all. Some Rottweiler bitches do not want to be mated, either by any dog or by particular dogs. There is every indication that hereditary factors underlie this behavior. Little is known about its nature or transmission.

A bitch that only lets itself be mated with the utmost difficulty had a son which also failed to mate (did not persevere). The sons of a dog imported from Sweden that was bad at mating did not mate or only with great difficulty (with the owner helping and intervening); mostly recourse was had to artificial insemination. Among the female descendants of this dog there was a strikingly large number of births by caesarian section. A dog's inability to mate is probably not an independent phenomenon, but one of the ways in which a complex of serious abnormalities finds expression. For this reason artificial insemination in dogs is a fatal course of action against which one cannot warn too strongly. The use of this method of fertilizing a bitch is highly inadvisable. The

Rottweiler bitch shows a wide variation as far as the appropriate day for mating is concerned. There are bitches which must be mated on the ninth day, and others where a mating will not succeed until the twenty-first day.

6. Character and behavior

The average Rottweiler

The Rottweiler Standard describes the ideal representative (which does not actually exist) of the breed. In these pages a description is attempted of the (equally non-existant) average Rottweiler. The terminology customary in the dog world is employed; later in the chapter better terms will be used which are drawn from the science of animal behavior.

The breed standard is not very clear on the subject of character. What the qualities named involve in terms of correct behavior is not explained. Nor is there any explanation of how behavior can be measured or where the line is drawn between desirable and undesirable behavior. If we attempt, despite this lack of clarity, to make a comparison with the behavior of the average Rottweiler, we see a number of differences.

The complex of qualities - self-confidence, courage and fearlessness - is not quite so pronounced in the average Rottweiler as in the dog described in the standard, no doubt because the environment in which many young Rottweilers grow up certainly does not make for the full exploitation of all the possibilities offered by this genetic endowment.

Temperament and desire for exercise are described in the standard as average. This is incorrect; the need for exercise is relatively small. Fifteen kilometers a day trotting alongside a bicycle is enough. Here the Rottweiler contrasts strongly with dogs such as Pointers, Setters and Dalmatians which need at least three times as much. As far as mental agility is concerned, the Rottweiler is dour, slow and rather obstinate. His perseverance and tenacity are indeed great; this is closely linked with his slowness to learn. He is not soon discouraged and has a certain inclination to take things easy. In training circles he is often said to have the sort of mentality which says 'if I don't come today, I may well come tomorrow'. What he remembers - and this follows logically from the foregoing - he retains for a long time. His attitude is either not particularly great or very selective; he will very quickly spot an approaching rival. He reacts little to sounds (unless they have a meaning for him); hardly any Rottweiler is afraid of gunshots.

The docility of the average Rottweiler is not very great; among adult males particularly we encounter very obstinate and bossy specimens. The differences in this respect between individuals and especially between the sexes are considerable. The sight of a ring with adult male Rottweilers at a show causes an unprejudiced bystander to entertain some doubts about their peaceable and obedient character. Gleaming teeth, murderous lunges and handlers (the word 'masters' is best avoided in this context) hauling desperately at leads offer an unusual sight.

Intolerance between male dogs, the constant urge to dominate is probably attributable in part to environmental factors. The average Rottweiler is thus noticeably less docile than the dog in the standard (which has average to great docility). In an earlier Dutch translation of the Rottweiler standard the word 'Führigkeit' (docility) was rendered as 'leadership', a mistake which was indeed more in agreement with the reality. The behavior of the Rottweiler dog towards bitches is as it should be - never aggressive. The Rottweiler is not inclined to be distrustful, possibly because of his mental slowness and not very high level of attention. The description in the standard of his sharpness (the tendency to react in a hostile way to external stimuli) is correct: less than average. But here too there are considerable variations. Dogs which are fearless and really sharp are not often met with in the case of the Rottweiler; very fearless dogs are often not very sharp. The few dogs that are sharp are often inclined to be insecure. In Germany it has never been known for dogs to be judged unsuitable for breeding because of excessive sharpness; in these cases they generally speak of 'gesunde Naturschärfe'. In Switzerland this certainly did happen a few years ago. A three year old dog was ruled out for being dangerously sharp, motivelessly aggressive and repeatedly threatening his owner.

The idea of fighting instinct referred to in the standard is difficult to define in terms of specific behavior. Most Rottweilers take pleasure in rough play and like to use their teeth. If their master is threatened they will give support; particularly if the threat is accompanied by a lot of action. Their mental hardness (the ability to be not easily influenced by unpleasant experiences) is great, again as a consequence of slowness to learn. The Rottweiler is not very vigilant, because he is not inclined to be distrustful, and for the same reason he does not bark much.

His stimulus threshold is high; a lot has to happen before he gets excited. This leads to a considerable degree of equilibrium. His balance is not easily disturbed and the disturbance does not last very long. It is known that in training the Rottweiler is not very ready to bite and soon gives up. He only goes through with the biting (holding fast) as long as it is a question of action and movement. Once the man in the padded suit stands still, much of the fun goes out of the game and he is released.

The Rottweiler has a well-developed sense of smell and he can be trained to be an outstanding tracking dog. He is not particularly keen on retrieving, although there are considerable variations in this respect.

The average Rottweiler is often peaceable and friendly with people, but his intolerance towards others of his own kind is considerable.

As a result of his dominating character the adult male dog often seeks a confrontation with other males, especially when they take an assertive position.

He is very affectionate, likes to be near his master and loves to be fondled. This sometimes makes him rather clinging. One finds this behavior in all types of Rottweilers, even to the toughest and most fearless individuals. Dogs with broad compact heads are much more inclined towards this rather 'immature' behavior than those with long heads. It is a question here of the retention of juvenile characteristics; dogs with broad heads have a physical shape which is usually met with only in puppies. Puppies are cared for by their mother and evoke caring behavior from her. Dogs with short heads have not only the typical appearance of a puppy but also the remnants of its behavior, and often try to evoke this caring behavior from their owners. Hereditary factors play a part in this.

Over thirty years ago Lorenz outlined the so-called 'baby model' and showed that people who keep household pets in order to be able to pamper them choose species, varieties or breeds with a high forehead, relatively large eyes and a short muzzle.

Owing to the physical changes which have taken place in the Rottweiler in recent decades (skull strongly instead of moderately arched, eyes mostly round and bulging instead of almond-shaped, muzzle considerably shorter, broader and less pointed), his appearance has come to show ever greater conformity with this model. His behavior has undergone a comparable development towards a high degree of attachment and affection. This makes him even less suitable than other dogs to spend a great deal of time alone in a kennel. An essential characteristic of domestic animals is that they have no flight distance and hardly any critical distance (overstepping the flight distance gives rise to flight behavior in the wild animal, and overstepping the critical distance leads to an attack). In addition many animal species have a 'personal territory'. We still find this in certain breeds of dog, but it is absent in the Rottweiler. Young wolves are willing to lie together, but when they are about six months old they will refuse to sleep closer than one meter away from a companion. Many dogs retain the youthful behavior of the wolf and readily sleep in close proximity to fellow members of the pack. The value placed on this behavior is a question of personal taste.

The average Rottweiler has little inclination to work; to ask him to do things which do not engage his interest (at that particular moment) is very difficult and makes it necessary to put pressure on him. This lack of inclination to work is possibly the result of too great a degree of mental hardness, insufficient docility and too little temperament.

Whether his power of endurance is really so great is difficult to ascertain. He does not easily allow himself to be pushed to the limits of his capacity. He is particularly keen on swimming and is very fond of children. The question is whether we may expect this (desirable) behavior from every kennel dog. He almost never shows flight and avoidance behavior; he is rarely jumpy. A well socialized Rottweiler will gladly seek contact, including contact with people outside his circle of acquaintance and especially with children. Whether he is bound to a particular territory depends on how he has been brought up. Extreme aggression rarely occurs, though there is some variation in this respect and the differences between the sexes are again great.

The Rottweiler does not bark much, even in the car. He usually likes car journeys, just as he likes eating. He usually goes into a deep trance over his dish, awakening only when he finds that the dish, for some incomprehensible reason, is completely empty. His desire for food can be extremely strong; it is no easy matter to get something edible out of a Rottweiler's mouth. As this can sometimes be necessary, it is advisable to get him accustomed to it as early as possible.

It is shocking how the anecdotes about the Rottweiler have changed over the years. They may serve to illustrate the nature of the changes which have occurred in the breed or perhaps in its owners.

There are recent stories about Rottweilers employed as police dogs which set about wrongdoers resisting arrest in such a way that a month in hospital becomes necessary or which, set free in a room in which there are Hell's Angels armed with helmets, iron bars and chains compel them to dive out through closed windows.

Stories, therefore, in which violence predominates. Earlier the emphasis was more on resoluteness and a certain insight.

An example (Kiel, 1910). A policeman lets his Rottweiler out and goes to a cafe where 14 drunken sailors are occupied in smashing the place up. Man and dog go inside and are met with blows and

77

shouting. Inside a minute the dog has put four sailors on the floor without injuring them significantly; the rest shrink back and let themselves be arrested without difficulty.

This feat of arms received national recognition in Germany, and the policeman and his dog were presented to the brother of Emperor William, Admiral Prince Henry of Prussia. The latter wanted to stroke the dog, and the policeman exclaimed in alarm: 'Don't come any closer, your Highness. The dog bites anyone that touches him without respect of persons. Please allow me to sit down and take off my helmet'. When this had been done, he said: 'Your Highness can stroke the dog now that I am off duty'.

Although the Rottweiler has lost part of his good qualities of behavior, for example his high intelligence, he is still - provided he is from a good line and has been well brought up - a dog with a particularly pleasant character.

Behavior in general

Behavior is not something separate and autonomous, but an adjustment, never completely successful, of the organism to its environment. This adjustment is controlled by the central nervous system which determines what behavior will be carried out. The senses supply information to the central nervous system about the situation in and around the body. The manner in which this information is processed and the kind of behavior to which it leads depend on the largely hereditary constitution of the central nervous system and on the experiences acquired and registered in the course of life. To put it another way, behavior is the result of a system of information processing. The structure of the central nervous system determines the manner in which the information processing is carried out, its result and thus - in broad terms - behavior.

The central nervous system is composed of a large number of switching units which are bound together to form a complicated network. The switching units are the nerve cells which consist of a round cell body with two kinds of offshoots: a number of short ones called dendrites and a long one called the axon or nerve fiber. Switching networks are formed by fibers from the nerve cells making contact with each other. The synapses at the ends of the nerve fibers fit on to the upper surface of the dendrites or the body of the other nerve cells. They provide for the transmission of signals and in part for the storage of information. The placing of the synapse on the receptor cell also determines how easily it activates the nerve cell. If it is on the cell body itself, the result is better than if it is on the far end of a dendrite.

This network of nerve cells forms the control appartus of behavior. The pattern of this switching system provides the explanation of a large part of the pattern of behavior. This complex structure evolves in accordance with a blueprint which is already present at conception. Its ultimate form and functioning are partly influenced by environmental factors in youth. In this there is a decisive interaction between hereditary constitution, stimuli from the environment and also suitable feeding. The brain develops in two stages. First the total number of nerve cells is built up; this happens early in gestation. Then the auxiliary cells develop, followed by the production of the insulating material which surrounds the nerve fibers along which the nerve cells send their messages. The first months in a dog's life form a most important but vulnerable period for the develogment of the brain.

A shortage of environmental stimuli or of food has no effect on the number of nerve cells. There may well be an effect on the formation of auxiliary cells, the insulation of the nerve fibers, the diameter of the nerve fibers and the number of synapses which can come to be 40 per cent below the maximum attainable. In addition the enzyme balance will be upset and the functioning of the synapses will be impaired. This has important consequences for the quality of the switching network. The transmission of signals may be less efficient, with greater risk of disturbance. The maximum loading, and the period during which maximum loading can be sustained without damage, are adversely affected. Short circuiting will occur sooner and the reliability of the network may be reduced, with the result that, for instance, in stress situations there is no access to memory data in specific areas.

Safety mechanisms, buffers and filter systems whose object is to guard against the overloading of the network may function less well. The possibility of the rapid dissipation of tension which is so necessary may become too limited, with the result that damage can easily be done to the organism The importance of these matters must not be underestimated, because the quality of the switching network determines the quality (and also the relevance and comprehensibility) of behavior.

If the second stage of development has passed and the period of rapid growth of the brain is over, there is no possibility of any further change.

Under-nourished experimental animals show social disturbances and a lowered reaction threshold, as a result of which they are more quickly irritated. Under-nourished children are linguistically backward, inferior in forming verbal concepts and less popular with classmates during their school days. Under-nourishment does not make them intellectually backward if the environment provides adequate stimulation. Hence the formation of the switching network is decisively influenced by the type and number of environmental stimuli. In this important period environmental influences not only determine the information which is stored in the brain but also leave their mark on the anatomical structure.

The offshoots of the brain cells grow differently. In this period it is determined how many connections are formed and with which other cells. This explains why use can only be made later of the kind of information experienced in earliest youth. In addition, the hormone reactions in adulthood which also determine behavior are partly fixed by the earliest youthful impressions. The cerebral cortex is so constructed that it can function at maximum efficiency in the environment perceived in earliest youth. Later information from the outside world leads to hardly any new connections between the brain cells, but is stored as memory.

During growth the dog often reacts selectively to environmental stimuli. With the development of social behavior, stimuli from others of the same species often seem to have more effect than

By making young dogs eat together from a large piece of meat, sharpness over food is reduced.

Concentration on chewing.

Flash von der Meierei VH III (Brutus vom Georgshof x Bärbel vom Grevingsberg). Declared valuable for breeding by the ADRK.

Axel vom Leitgraben VH III (Mirko von der Solitude x Fed. Ch. Cora vom Lindeck). A dog which, through his son, *Einar van het Brabantpark,* and his grandson, *Nino van de Brantsberg,* has had a great influence on Dutch Rottweiler breeding.

Arras van de Barrot (Simson van de Brantsberg x Anoushka van de Klankert).

Fed. Ch. 1970-1971-1972 *Falko vom Grünsfeld, VH III,* (Worad vom Jakobsbrunnen x Capra von der Chaussee).
Declared valuable for breeding by the ADRK.

Maik vom Rodenstein, VH III, (Dolf vom Weiherbrünnele x Burga von der Berg-kirche). Declared valuable for Rottweiler breeding by the ADRK.

Edda vom Ingenhof, VH I, (Dux vom Stüffelkopf x Dedda vom Kursaal). Declared valuable for Rottweiler breeding by the ADRK.

other stimuli. The influence is greatest in the critical periods. When this phase is over and the development of the cerebral cortex is complete, the susceptibility to influence diminishes. The pattern then formed can no longer be altered. Hence the saying, 'never too old to learn' does not always hold good.

The dog is not an animal that has all sorts of automatic behavior patterns, and it is therefore heavily involved in gathering information. The memory data are acquired in part genetically and in part by means of learning processes. Which learning processes are possible is determined by the hereditary make-up, and which of them takes place is at the same time determined by the environment. The operation of hereditary factors or behavior comes into being through different structures such as the nervous system, the functioning of hormones and the metabolic processes. The environment influences the predisposition of a behavior trait, but has no uniform influence on genetically different individuals.

In the scientific study of behavior a quite different terminology is used from that used in the dog world (in so far as the latter concerns itself with behavior). In the study of behavior the talk is, among other things, of the structural organization of behavior and of behavior systems. By a behavior system is meant a group of casually related actions. In the case of dogs distinctions are drawn between systems for threat and fight behavior, submission and flight behavior, sexual behavior, etc.

If we now assume that every behavior system has a close relationship with a part of the switching network of nerve cells, it will be clear that the stronger the link between different parts of the network, the easier it will be for the behavior systems to influence each other. If in a situation which has activated the system for fight behavior, a change appears which gives rise to flight behavior then, with very little linkage between the relevant parts of the network, this will lead at first to strong aggression changing abruptly to strong flight behavior.

If there is a harmonious link between the behavior systems, then in the same situation a moderate degree of threat will be shown which, as the situation alters, passes to a moderate degree of avoidance. In the first case behavior proceeds completely from the one system, changing suddenly to the behavior of another system. In the second case, only a part is carried out of the behavior appropriate to both systems, and the transition between them is gradual. This is a characteristic of balanced behavior. It is caused by good integration of behavior systems and a harmonious linkage of the partial networks in the central nervous system.

The latter, as previously stated, is influenced both by heredity and by environment.

However good the hereditary disposition of a dog may be, his behavior will not develop normally in the absence of specific environmental conditions. He needs the social interaction of growing up with others of his own species and with man. Without this, serious behavior aberrations ensue. The ethologist 't Hart compares this social interaction with the taking of food. To be able to develop normally a body must be provided regularly with suitable food. If food is lacking and the body does not develop normally, it cannot be concluded from this that the ultimate structure of the body is not genetically determined. Social interaction is for behavior the same as food is for the body: an indispensable condition for the carrying out of the genetic program.

Environmental influences between conception and birth
The immediate environment of the unborn offspring of a living being consists in the first instance of its mother, the environment in the mother and the composition of the food which is received via the placenta.

The environment in the mother (blood and other organic substances) are affected by the processes that take place in the mother's body, particularly by the secretion of hormones which reach the embryo through the blood. The youthful experiences of an animal have a great influence on its development, and the influences of experiences during the formation of the body is at least as great. The emotions of the mother during pregnancy form a part of the experience of the unborn young.

Thus it has been shown that the offspring of rats which are subjected during pregnancy to stimuli arousing fear bear the marks of it throughout their lives. They are much more timid than animals born of mothers which did not experience any fear at all during pregnancy.

This was also the case when they were not suckled and reared by their own mother, but by mothers which had not undergone the fear arousing stimuli. Similar experiments have been carried out with guinea pigs. When male hormones were administered to the female in the middle stage of pregnancy, their female offspring showed typical masculine shape and masculine behavior.

It was also found that the offspring of rats which were handled with a certain regularity during pregnancy were considerably less sensitive than those of rats to which this did not happen. This was so both when they stayed with their own mother and when they were handed over to a foster-mother. The fondling of pregnant mice led to bigger litters and an increase in the number of survivng young.

Non-genetic transmission of behavior

The imitation of the mother's behavior in particular is an important factor influencing behavior.

Bitches that are nervous, often showing flight behavior (leaving the outside run and retreating into the kennel when they see a stranger), will communicate this behavior to puppies in their near neighborhood, even when they are not their own puppies or are those of another breed.

Extremely timid bitches which ought not actually to have been bred from at all should not be left too long with their puppies, unless they are not in a position to display their bad behavior characteristics. If there is a good dog nearby with steady and fearless behavior, this will produce a more favorable effect. Breeders should not punish their bitches seriously or force submissive behavior upon them when puppies are present. During the period when puppies are growing up the relationship between breeder and bitch should be pleasant and relaxed.

Critical periods and periods of anxiety in the dog

Profound research has been carried out into the consequences of youthful experiences in the dog for the development of behavior. The fact has emerged that environmental stimuli have a particularly big influence. The absence of particular experiences leads to behavior disturbances later on.

The period of youth can be divided up as follows:

a. Vegetative phase (weeks 1-2). The brain is far from fully grown, and the puppy is blind and deaf. The senses of touch and taste are moderately developed, the feeling of balance strongly so. The puppy reacts to only a limited number of stimuli. Around the twelfth day the first attempts are made to walk unassisted;

b. Transitional phase (week 3), in which sight and hearing develop strongly;

c. First phase of socialization or imprinting (weeks 4-7), in which under the influence of environmental stimuli the brain develops rapidly. About the beginning of the fourth week the puppy can hear effectively and playful fighting begins. The tail is wagged for the first time in the fourth week;

d. Second or true phase of socialization (weeks 8-12);

e. Pecking order phase (weeks 13-16);

f. Pack order phase (weeks 17-25);

g. Puberty (week 26 - sexual maturity).

The imprinting phase (imprinting is a rapid learning process in which species awareness is acquired) and a part of the socialization phase form a critical period. This critical period, characterized by a special aptitude for learning, begins on the eighteenth and ends on the sixty-fifth day. The beginning of this period is marked by the increased inclination and the ability to flee (walking improves and immobility diminishes).

The socialization process falls into three phases. After the imprinting phase just mentioned, in which acquaintance is made with people and other dogs, comes the true socialization phase. In this the young dog gets to know people and other dogs as fellow-members of the pack with which play and other forms of interaction are possible. In addition there is the period up to six months in which the socialization effect must be maintained and strengthened. The result of this is that what has been learned is not forgotten and is retained throughout life. It is the so-called instability of retention of young animals which makes this necessary.

If a dog does not have sufficient contact with people between the third and seventh weeks of his life, timidity and fearfulness will be the result. He will fail to develop the ability to form a bond with human beings and to restrain the inclination of the wild animal to run away. The more contacts a dog has in this period with people, with other dogs, with other animals and with objects, in short the more he is involved, the more inclined he will be in later life to well-balanced behavior.

'Contact' is not just a matter of seeing or hand-feeding. Smell, touch, skin contact and above all play are of vital importance. The dog must be fondled a good deal, and have the opportunity to become thoroughly familiar with the scent of man. Puppies, just like children, need love and attention. They have a pronounced need of affection.

If the dog has exclusive contact with people and none, or not enough, with other dogs, this will result in inappropriate behavior towards others of his own species (timidity, aggression, sexual malfunction). If the young dog has contact only with women, he will show a certain reserve towards men. It is also of the greatest importance that a young male dog in this phase should have contact with small children (naturally under supervision, so that children cannot cause the dog to acquire an aversion to them). This early contact reinforces the inhibition against biting small children later on.

Where the young dog has not become attached to man by the fifth week, problems will arise with rearing, with instilling obedience and eventually with training.

If a young dog is left too long with his mother, or if a boring environment compels him to be too much occupied with her, the result will be excessive dependence. This is not to say that mother and puppies should be separated from each other as much as possible (this too leads to traumas if it happens too soon), but rather that a young dog over 5 weeks should make his bed where sufficient diversion is offered. Toys and an interesting environment will see to it that the contacts between mother and puppies become looser by themselves.

If contacts between man and dog are considerably less in the imprinting phase than those between dog and dog, the resulting poverty of contacts will cause the dog to become anti-social, reserved and unapproachable. To repeat, playing, romping and fondling are of the greatest importance, really just as important as food and water.

Another important period with an irreversible learning process in which the absence of particular environmental influences leads to undesirable behavior later on is that in which the dog is introduced to unfamiliar places. This period is between the third and fifth months.

If the young dog is not taken frequently to different places which are new to him, he will always be afraid of unfamiliar places. Lack of, or lack of sufficient, confrontation with strange noises can also lead to him becoming hypersensitive to them.

The first critical period affects steadiness of behavior towards people, the second towards places.

In the early part of a young dog's life there are two periods of emotional instability in which impressions of anxiety can easily be formed. These periods of anxiety are connected with major physical changes. The first period of anxiety occurs between the eighth and the tenth week and is comparable with that of the human child around eight months. In this period nothing new is done with the dog and psychic and physical traumas are avoided. Physical punishment is even more wrong than at other times, seeing that the dog's ability to withstand stress is limited in this phase of its life and the after-effects will be considerable.

Social animals imitate the behavior of those of higher, rather than lower rank; confrontation of a young dog at a sensitive period with physical violence from one of the higher rank can lead to aggressive behavior. Visits to the vet are also avoided during this period, and in the same way the dog is not locked up, isolated or left. The tattooing of numbers in ears should have been done before this period starts.

After the tenth week adaptability has increased in such a way that these experiences can be more easily withstood. In addition, the social and emotional links which have by then been formed with other dogs and with the owner contribute greater possibilities for the reduction of stress.

The best period of all for socialization between dog and master (as distinct from human beings in general) is between the tenth and twelfth weeks. If a dog comes to his master in the sixth week of life, this can lead to the formation of a strong bond between them. Socialization takes place in part before the first period of anxiety. This period is endured reasonably well because the bond already formed between man and dog allows him a certain release of tension and leaves few traces behind. The period of anxiety can reinforce the socialization effect because for the sake of relief from stress the puppy seeks support from his master.

If the puppy comes to his master at eight weeks, the first period of anxiety begins with a very radical change in his life. This increases the risk that this period will have after-effects. The possibility of stress reduction is not great because social and emotional bonds are lacking; the socialization process may be weakened and the period will be less well endured.

If the move to the final home takes place between the tenth and twelfth weeks, the period of anxiety will be born without problems. The environment is very familiar and the bonds with the mother and the rest of the litter ensure maximum reduction of anxiety. A longer stay can lead - once maturity has been reached - to greater tolerance of other dogs, but also to a certain poverty of contact in relation to people. One should therefore provide for plenty of contact with people to ensure that socialization does not remain incomplete.

Around the age of five months there is a second period of anxiety. Even when the dog is well socialized and has no fear of strangers, strong reactions can arise to changes in the environment. In this period of emotional instability, too, the dog should be spared unpleasant experiences.

Play behavior
The play of the young dog is of great significance for the development of behavior in later life. Play is a form of active learning, and the two things have a common basis. In animals the relationship between prolonged youth, much play and high intelligence is very clear. Play and youthful experience lead to a harmonious integration of the different behavior systems. The elements of the behavior systems appear in an arbitrary sequence, and the motivation of the activated system (e.g., aggression, flight, sexuality) is low. In play the animal learns quickly. New possibilities are discovered and tried out. Through the low motivation the organism can take a more detached view of things. Failure in a play situation does not lead to any loss or injury. It may be assumed that one of the functions of play is to guard the organism against rigidity and so leave room for innovation.

Play behavior only takes place when the primary needs for food, warmth and rest have been satisfied and the animal is free from anxiety. In the play of the young dog emtional bonds are forged and socialization is reinforced. Puppies need group play and social interaction in order to have normal sexual behavior later on. A dog that has never played with others in his youth will never feel at home with them later. Cooperation is also learned through play. Anyone who wants to train his dog will have to play with him at an early stage. Play also determines the social relationships of dominance and subordination. Young dogs must have the opportunity early in their lives to establish a clear ranking. Where this is so, the chance of conflict (this applies throughout life) is small. In mock fights the puppy exercises himself and learns to know his own skill and strength. From this evolve naturally the rules which prevent injury to his fellows, so that the social bonds are not weakened. The restraint on biting is of great importance for dogs which will have to be accepted into a community of people. Young dogs must be able to play with all kinds of objects. They gain from this the ability to control their bodies and movement and to be independent of the mother. Toys also assist interaction with other members of the litter.

If a bitch wants to play with her puppies, she should not be prevented. Her possibly rough play will stimulate the puppies to stand up for themselves and help them to be self-confident and unafraid.

The enriched environment

There is no fundamental difference between the surroundings in which a wolf living in the wild is born and those in which he matures and spends the rest of his life. His gradually developing senses enable him bit by bit to become acquainted with his surroundings, and his relatively prolonged youth ensures that the growing organism has the chance to adapt itself to the number and types of stimuli presented. Thus the young wolf develops precisely to the extent and in the direction which make possible an optimum adaptation to the environment.

The natural environment presents a diversity of stimuli: a bird suddenly flying overhead, an unexpected shower of rain, the sun appearing from behind a cloud and casting shadows, the cry of an animal, ground which is hard or soft, dry or damp, bushes with or without thorns - in short, anything at all apart from dust, newspapers and artificial light. The natural environment is characterized by many different sudden and drastic changes. The dog's central nervous system is not only capable of learning to deal with those multifarious stimuli, but actually needs them to come to full development.

The environment in which most domestic dogs spend the first eight weeks of their lives is poor in stimuli, and the stimuli which it provides are different from those provided by the environment of the fully grown dog. This is unfavorable for the development of behavior, because part of the dog's potential is not used and, despite his prolonged youth, he does not develop in the direction which would bring about the greatest possible adaptation to the mature environment.

The dog ends up in an environment in which he has not been able to install himself during the vital early phases of his youth; he is confronted there with stimuli which are quite different in scale and character from any to which he has been accustomed.

With the wild dog the rate of development of the sense organs determines the degree to which he becomes acquainted with environmental stimuli; in the domestic dog the sense organs develop in surroundings which are stimulus-poor. Consequently they develop less, but after about eight weeks, when the dog changes owners, an immense change of surroundings suddenly takes place and the young dog is faced very abruptly with the stimuli with which he will have to deal for the rest of his life.

With dogs whose nervous system is inherently not so good, this can give rise to problems in later life. The many and various stimuli can lead to stresses which cannot, or can only with difficulty, be released and the result may be 'short circuitry'.

It is no exaggeration to say that it is of the utmost importance -for both dog and master - that the youthful environment should resemble as much as possible that of maturity.

Another difference between the natural and kennel environment concerns the type and number of the social relationships which the young animal has. A young wolf generally grows up not only with his mother and his litter brothers and sisters, but also with his father and possibly with and uncle or aunt and perhaps an elder brother or sister. This gives rise to a wide spectrum of social contacts.

A young dog grows up with his mother and with his litter brothers and sisters with whom he is constantly together as a rule. Generally the bitch is not allowed to occupy herself with rearing the young over a long period, but even when this is the case the puppy does not have any contact with an adult male dog. The consequences of this are difficult to judge. Does it increase the tendency of the dog to grow up to be a 'mother's boy'? Or does it lead to disobedience, less willingness to accept a subordinate position, intolerance of male dogs, perhaps even refractoriness at a later period in life. Or perhaps all these things at once? The impoverished kennel environment also causes an undesirable prolongation of mother-child dependence. A way to reduce or prevent the undesirable mother fixation is the presence of a friendly male dog who knows the social code (everything is allowed to puppies and they are never bitten).

A means of avoiding the drawbacks of stimulus-poverty in kennel conditions is offered by the enriched environment. The concept emanates from the American institutions for the study of animal behavior, in which it was observed how much the stimulus-poor laboratory surroundings of animals kept there restricted the development of their behavior. In the enriched environment more, and more varied, stimuli are deliberately provided than in the average kennel environment, and the play behavior of puppies is stimulated. The aim is to use the potential of the animal as much as possible and to enable him to acquire flexibility in dealing with all kinds of stimuli. This makes possible a high degree of adaptation to the stimuli-rich environment of adult life. In an enriched environment the sense organs are stimulated, first especially balance and the senses which involve contact (taste, smell and touch), and later also those that operate at a distance (sight and hearing). At the same time all kinds of steps are taken to stimulate the integration of behavior systems.

For the new-born puppy this means in concrete terms:

a. Letting him often take the scent of people and of objects of all kinds;

b. A great deal of handling, carrying and stroking.

For the somewhat older puppy the possibilities are extended to:

a. Letting him hear different sounds (switching the radio on and off, vacuum cleaner, lawn mower);

b. Placing new objects every day in his immediate surroundings;

c. Giving him a regular opportunity to get to know a different environment (even if only other rooms in the house). The first critical period also has an influence, though not as marked, on the behavior of the dog towards places;

d. Equipping the area in which the puppies live with chests, boxes, a shallow trough of water (if the temperature allows and there is no danger to the puppies), tires, pails without bottoms (tunnels), brushes, washing-up mops or pieces of cloth hanging on strings, a see-saw of appropriate size with a bell, a trampoline (metal bed springs), in short anything that squeaks, turns and moves.

e. Hanging up within the field of vision large cloths of all colors which move in the wind.

Adequate space is also important; a young dog must be able to choose for himself whether to lie close beside his mother or the rest of the litter. Usually this is what he will do, but he must not be forced to do so by lack of room and hence take longer to establish his independence.

As long as the influencing of behavior is carried out with the kind of household articles named here, there is no risk of adverse effects. If one goes in for swings and other devices which make it impossible for the puppy to get away, caution is advised.

An excess of stimuli may indeed result in blunting and reducing the learning capacity. Application of the enriched environment to dogs has shown that their motor ability develops more quickly and that coordination in standing and walking is improved at an early stage; the puppies show a dominant type of behavior, are more active and mobile, less nervous at the approach of stangers, perform better in situations in which there is a problem to be solved, are less fearful and panicky, and more inquisitive.

No information is available about the optimum dosage of the different kinds of stimuli (this is likely to vary according to the breed). Probably the best kind of enriched environment for young Rottweilers in a box is the kind of domestic interior seen in paintings by Jan Steen in which people chat, walk about and laugh, the radio and TV are on, and the puppies are stroked and now and then taken into the children's beds.

Then (fourth week) during the daytime a large run with a view of a street with all kinds of traffic and the associated noises; in the evening they go back into the house where they are played with as long as they like. Every few days a car ride to a new place (beach, woods, heath, sand-dunes). Now and then they are carried through the center of a town or village (market, department store). This results in the young dog being constantly occupied and able to learn and try out new things. The new and exciting experiences will stimulate their learning ability. The nervous system will develop well. This and the information gained by it will stand the dog in good stead in later life.

The enriched environment does not however provide the solution to every problem. It merely attempts to make use of all the inherited aptitudes which are usually greater than one realizes. But when the aptitude for a certain type of behavior is extremely poor, then even the enriched environment will fail.

An example of this is the attempt to reduce nervousness in a breed of Pointers. This behavior appeared to be genetically determined to such an extent that both a limited use of the enriched environment technique and the fostering of puppies by non-nervous

93

bitches had scarcely any effect.

In the application of the enriched environment, the excitation of the sense of touch by means of skin stimulation occupies a special place. Touch is the oldest and most important of the senses, without which life is impossible. The skin is extremely important, not ony for physical functions but also for the development of behavior. Through skin stimulation it is possible to influence the spinal nerves and other parts of the central nervous system.

These stimuli bring about an increase in the sensory and motor activities in the internal organs, have an effect on the veins and capillary tubes and cause changes in hormone production.

In the development of any organism with a skin there are periods when the outer covering must be adequately stimulated if it is to develop in a normal manner.

A series of independently conducted experiments has shown how exceptionally clear are the consequences of early skin stimulation for behavior.

In the case of babies it has been proved that the nervous system requires to be supplied with stimuli through the skin in the early phase of establishing reflexes. The brain and nervous system of men, dogs and salamanders (to name just a few species) develop more quickly in reaction to skin stimulation. According to Montagu this is a basic need (like eating, drinking and sleep) of all vertebrates, though not of all invertebrates.

In rats, fondling has the greatest effect in the first ten days of life. In experiments 13 per cent of rats which had been regularly fondled died within 48 hours after an operation compared with 79 per cent of rats which had not been fondled. Gentle handling and fondling gives the nervous system greater stability and leads to quiet, friendly animals with a high level of resistance. Absence of such handling leads to nervous, irritable animals. If pregnant rats are prevented from licking themselves (skin stimulation), the milk glands develop 50 per cent less and litter fostering behavior is seriously disturbed.

Male rats, fondled from the 23rd to the 44th day, are considerably bigger and heavier. In a behavior test they show themselves much less nervous. Other researchers concluded that rats which are fondled during the first ten days of their lives become heavier, learn best, live longest, show less fear, are more spirited in investigating unfamiliar surroundings, have a greater brain weight (cerebral cortex and sub-cortex are more strongly developed), have a nervous system in a more advanced stage of development, show more liveliness, curiosity and problem-solving ability, show more inclination to dominate, grow more quickly (body and skeleton), make better use of their food, and have greater emotional stability and a better memory.

Skin stimulation in earliest youth has an exceptionally favorable effect on the immunological system; the ability to resist infection and other diseases increases strongly. In animals which have been fondled in youth the quantity of antibodies in the system is considerably greater.

Horses that are thoroughly handled immediately after birth develop exceptional maturity of behvior. Without being less manageable and easy to handle at other times, they show particularly 'responsible' behavior in emergency situations and resourcefulness in communicating with people. The annual death rate among children in a New York hospital fell by 75 per cent after the introduction of a maternity program in which the children were picked up, carried about and caressed.

Dog breeders must spend a lot of time stroking, carrying and handling puppies and taking them on their laps (the daily weighing, continued up to eight weeks, helps in this connection). This is another reason why one should always buy a dog from a small owner or breeder; in the dog factories they have neither the time nor the inclination to give the puppy the skin contact that he needs. The new owner of a young dog must allow ample time every day for brushing his companion. He should keep this up as long as possible, preferably until the end of the dog's life. The motto in horsy circles, 'well brushed is half fed', is also fully applicable to the dog.

In addition the young dog should be taken at an early stage (but *not* in the periods of anxiety) successively to shops, department stores, markets, villages or town centers, sports grounds, cinemas, pageants, fairgrounds, football matches, in lifts, trains, tram, bus, car, along busy roads (first with and later against the traffic), etc.

His master should ensure that the dog is confronted with the unkown in a friendly but quiet way. The dog must not associate new experiences with a master snarling and tugging at the lead. If the dog is afraid of something, his master goes and sits next to it and persuades the dog to come close, or else he picks the dog up and carries him quietly away. In so doing he puts the dog at his ease, pats him and speaks kindly to him. At this stage in which we are concerned with rearing, the dog should be disciplined as little as possible during the first three months. If he does something wrong, we divert his attention. When he begins to be taught that some things are not allowed, the word, 'No', must be followed not long after by a reassuring touch (stroke).

It is also important, in the interests of obedience, that around the twelfth week (and *not* later) the dog should be taught in a playful way to obey the command, 'Sit', and to fetch a ball or other article.

If the dog has a good disposition and the breeder has not gone too far wrong, this investment in time will give you a Rottweiler with particularly pleasant and steady behavior.

Problems with behavior

Complaints about dogs relate, in descending order of frequency, to the dirtying of the house, chewing the furniture and biting people. We are concerned here with the last of these problems, that of aggression. Aggression may be defined as 'threatening and combative behavior directed towards others of the species'. In this case we regard, for convenience, both dogs and people as members of the same species.

Aggression is generally provoked by concern for the young, territorial behavior, sexual motives, the overstepping of the critical distance, the establishment of rank order and jealousy over food. Jealousy over food is small in wolves, even when aggressiveness in the pack has increased because of prolonged lack of food. Food aggression in dogs is greater. A comparative study showed that in Standard Poodles, the young come last to the dish whereas in wolves they are the first to eat.

Both timidity and aggression may be related to poor socialization and inadequate integration of behavior systems.

Physical punishment in the first period of anxiety can be another cause of aggression. The administration of corporal punishment always increases the tendency towards aggression; the effect is the opposite of that intended. This occurs, not only through the frustration caused by this form of punishment, but also through the fact that a social being is inclined to imitate the behavior of a superior rather than that of an inferior. Forms of punishment other than corporal punishment should therefore always be preferred.

Aggressive behavior can be aroused by external stimuli such as the sight of a rival, but also by non-specific frustrating factors such as set-backs, obstacles, disappointments, heat, hunger, boredom, idleness and an excess of energy. Also hormonal factors and an increase in the substances catecholamine and indolamine in the blood may accentuate the tendency to show aggressive behavior. A reduction may be brought about by administration of dextroamphetamine and, in the case of male dogs by the (barbarous) method of castration.

Frustration may also be caused and aggression increased by loneliness, emotional deprivation, too little freedom of movement, too little space and constant confinement. It appears that in breeds such as the Old English Sheepdog, the hair hanging over the eyes causes a constant irritaion of the retina which can lead to aggression. Clipping away the hair is the remedy indicated in this case.

Misunderstanding on the part of dog owners as to a dog's essential needs is the cause of much aggression. The dog has a strong need to feel himself part of a group. For a healthy, well-fed dog this is the strongest need of all.

The extent to which dogs react against restriction on their freedom varies. Pavlov speaks in this connection of the 'innate freedom reflex'. This is most easily produced in dogs that are highly susceptible to stimuli. Constant sitting behind doors, fences and windows causes tensions, particularly in dogs with a low stimulus threshold and a strong innate freedom reflex. People on the other side of these barriers can become 'hate objects', and if an opportunity occurs to get at them they can be bitten.

It is not surprising that nearly all cases of serious aggression by dogs against people concern dogs kept in kennels.

As the threshold level for factors causing frustration is regulated by nerves or hormones, the tendency to carry out aggressive behavior may fluctuate.

A learning process also plays a part in aggression. One must start early to teach the dog not to behave aggressively. It is important to prevent aggression or to stop a young dog from carrying out aggressive behavior (by picking him up and putting him down quietly somewhere else). By making a young dog 'sharp' (e.g., at the food dish) the threshold of aggression is lowered, with the result that later on a smaller stimulus is enough to elicit aggressive behavior. Very independent or dominant puppies, or puppies with a low stimulus threshold, will be very likely to bite later in stress situations.

Such dogs become problem cases if they are placed in an environment which - to use another term of Pavlov's - strongly stimulates their active defensive reflex.

The playful teasing of this kind of puppy can lead to difficulties when the dog reaches maturity. Frequent lifting and carrying of puppies - beginning at birth and continuing until they are less helpless at around three months - makes them very ready to be submissive. We see the same thing in the case of people; from birth to about 14 month a child is fairly helpless and is carried everywhere by its parents. The young child experiences a relationship of dependence and, as a result, forms a strong habit of passivity towards older people. Even when they are grown up, it rarely happens that children use physical violence against their parents.

With many dogs the problems with aggression start when they are two years old. Readiness to defend the territory then reaches its definitive level. To keep this in check, ample opportunity must be arranged for friendly meetings with strangers on the dog's home ground.

What sort of aggression is to be considered normal and what sort abnormal is not easy to decide. Trumler maintains that it is normal for a bitch that has had puppies to kill strange puppies. Not to do so points to a loss of instinct. On the other hand, a male dog that kills a puppy displays abnormal behavior because he should behave towards every puppy as if it were his own.

A normal male dog shows non-specific fostering behavior, whereas a bitch limits this to her own offspring.

There are examples in the literature of abnormal aggression in a number of breeds - the Cocker Spaniel, Alsatian, Corgi, Saint Bernard, Berner Sennenhund and others. In these cases the dog bites the owner or other members of the household without any warning. The hair stands on end, the pupils are enlarged and the expression is somewhat dazed. After the attack the dogs are once again nice and obedient.

In male dogs these attacks generally occur first when they are about 1½ years old. In bitches the phenomenon occurs less often, and when it does it starts later. The frequency and duration of the attacks increase. The dog starts 'defending' everything. There is a loss of social bonds; the dog regards the human members of his pack as strangers belonging to a species with which he is not socialized at all. So far no therapy for this has been developed; the problem is resolved by a usually untimely and final visit to the vet. The causes of this abnormal form of aggression, which does not occur in the Rottweiler, must be sought in inadequate socialization, a stimulus-poor environment in youth and a poor hereditary constitution which results in the effects of socialization diminishing by fits and starts and not being maintained at all in the long run.

There is a constant increase in the number of press reports about dogs that unexpectedly attack their masters. They give the dog world and pedigree dogs a bad name. If the present method of selection for breeding (by appearance) is not replaced by selection primarily on the basis of behavior, it will not be long before the dog represents a danger to public health. Not because of disease, infection and the like, but purely and simply because of unpredictable and uncontrollable aggression.

It ought to be possible to prevent a good deal of aggression if people knew more about matters to do with dogs and were more keenly observant.

Now dogs communicate in a different way from people. Information about their frame of mind is conveyed by signs. Here we must distinguish between distance-increasing and distance-reducing signs, ambivalent signs (in case of behavioral conflict) and non-specific signs. If every dog owner learned to understand the signs in the first category, many cases of biting would be preventable; every normal dog gives a visible and audible warning before biting.

As regards the visible demeanor, one must pay attention to:

a. The position of the ears;

b. The wrinkling of the forehead and muzzle;

c. The way in which the lips are held.

Fear is shown by the way the ears lie back and the dog pulls back the corners of the mouth. A wrinkled forehead denotes lack of fear, whereas wrinkles on the muzzle indicate that the dog is ready to show aggression.

As a domesticated animal the dog has no flight distance and - usually only in specific situations - few remains of a critical distance. In so far as the dog still has this, it amounts to about one meter. Usually the extent of a dog's inclination to bite is strongly determined by the extent to which his owner is also his master, in other words the extent to which his owner dominates him. The pack leader decides whether there is to be a fight or not. The dog that attacks without waiting when his master is present does not appear to recognize him as a superior.

The dog is a hunter living in a social group, a beast of prey with the largest brain in proportion to body size of all the domesticated animals. Enclosed within this sentence is the solution to almost all the problems that one can have with aggression in dogs.

Much aggression arises from an excess of energy; the result of this are irritability and an inclination to bite. Fifteen kilometers a day alongside a bicycle will put paid to that. The dog needs contact with other members of the pack; he must feel himself to be a part of a group in which there is a clear rank order. If the latter is lacking, he will try to create it for himself by confrontation. The dog needs to receive sufficient stumuli and impressions; this, too, is catered to by long walks and bicycle outings. The different forms of training can also help by providing him for a number of hours a week with a task in which he can fulfill himself.

Facial expression of the Rottweiler under the influences of uncertainty and fear. The dog's emotions can be read from his facial expression. From 1 to 4 and 7 uncertainty (fear or aggression) increases. The ears are laid back and the lips flattened in a submissive grin. From 1 to 2 and 3 readiness to attack increases. The ears and the corners of the mouth are brought forward and the lips raised. From 3 to 6 and 9 the signs of aggression are joined with those of uncertainty. Expression 9, in which 7 and 3 are combined, is typical of fear-biting (after Lorenz and Fox).

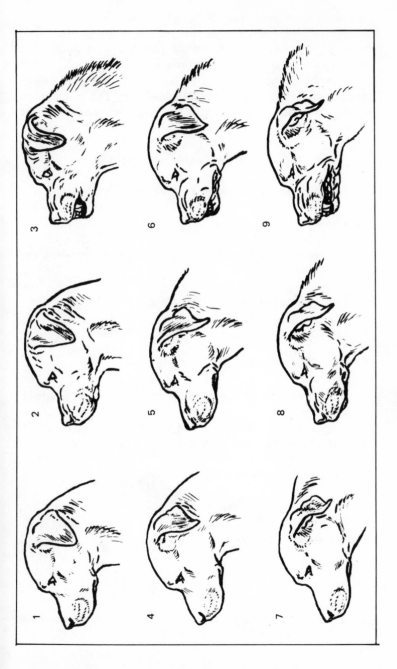

Reading list on behavior: to acquire some insight into the behavior of dogs and the factors which influence this, it is necessary to provide oneself with a foundation of theory and practical knowledge. Without working in this way scarcely more than superficial knowledge will be achieved in this field. which happens much in cases of assumed knowledge. The first step on the way to understanding lies in the thorough reading of the following books:

1. *Honden zijn om van te houden,* E. Trumler.

2. *De hond ernstig genomen,* E. Trumler.

3. *The Wolf,* L. D. Mech.

4. *Collegedictaat Diergedrag,* J. H. Frijlink, Universiteit van Amsterdam.

5. *Ethologie, de biologie van het gedrag,* Pudoc, Wageningen.

6. *De functie van het zenuwstelsel,* J. P. Schade.

7. *Abnormal behavior in animals,* M. Fox.

8. *Biological basis of human social behavior,* R. A. Hinde.

9. *Dog behavior* (oorspronkelijke titel: *Genetics and the social behavior of the dog*), J. P. Scott, J. L. Fuller.

10. *De tastzin,* A. Montagu.

11. *Guide dogs for the blind: their selection, development and training.* C. J. Pfaffenberg, J. P. Scott, J. L. Fuller, B. E. Ginsburg, S. W. Bielfelt.

7. Behavior Test For Mature Rottweilers

The behavior test of the Dutch Rottweiler Club

In 1972 the Dutch Rottweiler Club decided to set up a committee charged with developing a behavioral test, translating the requirements of the Rottweiler Standard as regards behavior into terms of specific behavior in test situations, conducting tests and expressing a judgment about the observed behavior.

The test that was developed, improved and adopted, consists of 3 sections and 14 sub-sections.

SECTION 1, in which the dog, the handler, the judges and the public are involved, consists of the following sub-sections:
1. Group
2. Stroking
3. Wide lane
4. Narrow lane
5. Objects
6. Slowly closing circle
7. Rapidly closing circle

SECTION 2, in which only the dog and the judges are involved, consists of:
8. Friendly people I
9. Slowly moving 'criminal'
10. Running 'criminal'
11. Threatening 'criminal'
12. Friendly people II

SECTION 3, in which the dog, the handler and the judge are involved, consists of:
13. Shots
14. Attack on master

NETHERLANDS ROTTWEILER CLUB

Name: ___MIRKO_____ NHSB ___774000___

Sire: ___Cuno vom Hause Kömmelt_____ dog/~~bitch~~

Dam: ___Tosca_____ D/Birth _26·10·_

Breeder: _A. J. Hulsman, Heino_____

Owner: ___J. E. Chardet-Alvares_____ Address: _Oude Utrechtsweg 12, Baarn_

Test: ___Kaatsheuvel_____ Date: ___15 May 1977_____

Further details_____

_____

Conclusions concerning behavior with the various tests:

-with master

(1-2)	stranger	friendly & calm
(3-4)	in street & lane	calm, attentive especially to master
(5)	near objects	little interest, calm
(6)	in slow circle	very much at ease
(7)	in fast circle	calm, well-balanced, imperturbable

-without master

(8)	friendly people	somewhat depressed, no fear
(9)	calm 'criminal'	alert, calm, no giving ground
(10)	fast 'criminal'	jumped at, barked, even grab
(11)	threatening 'criminal'	somewhat intimidated, gives ground a bit, comes back again
(12)	friendly man	friendly & joyful

-with master

(13)	shooting	attentive & calm
(14)	assault	watchful, then defending
(15)	xxxxxxx	

Space for remarks concerning sharpness, unpredictableness, jumpiness, liveliness, attentiveness.

He is very tuned to his master

xxxxxxxxxxxxxxxxxxxxxxxxxxxxxxxxxxxxxxxx
Entered on 31·12·77 in class: BA

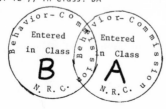

On behalf of the Behavior Commissi

H. J. ten Bruggencate

Form for conclusions concerning Behavior Test (Netherlands Rottweiler Club-N.R.C.

Explanation

The dog comes on the lead to the test area with his owner and walks through a group of about 20 people (test 1). In this and practically all the other tests no commands are given (from master to dog), and the lead is not held tight. The owner shakes hands with some of those present; the dog is stroked by the judges, if they are told that this is possible (test 2). In the group there is a 'criminal'; from the dog's reaction on seeing the 'criminal' walking beside him it is judged whether he is conditioned to this and knows the meaning of the padded suit.

The group arranges itself in two rows facing each other about three meters apart; handler and dog walk twice between them (test 3)

The rows move in to a distance of about one meter and the handler and the dog being tested again walk twice between them (test 4).

Then the rows return to the original position and handler and dog pass between them yet again, but this time:

a. An umbrella is opened;
b. A handkerchief is waved unexpectedly;
c. A closed box containing pebbles is flung down about 1½ meters in front of the dog;
d. At the end of the rows a folding chair is pulled over some distance in front of the dog by means of a piece of string (test 5).

Next those present form a circle (diameter 20 meters) with the owner and the dog being tested in the middle. Slowly, step by step, the circle closes round them (test 6).

Then the circle opens, resumes its original size, and closes again, but this time rapidly (test 7).

This concludes the first section.

In Section 2 the dog is left on his own in a place among trees where he is not visible to his owner or to the public. After being here alone for seven minutes the dog is approached by the judges. They speak to him in a friendly way and, if possible, try to stroke him (test 8).

When they have gone, the 'criminal' comes up to the dog, walking quietly, not speaking but staring straight at him, stops at a distance of one meter in front of the dog and goes away again (test 9). Then he repeats this, but this time at a not too rapid run (test 10).

This procedure is then repeated yet again, but now the 'criminal' shouts and makes threatening arm movements with a stick in his hand. At two meters distance from the dog he strikes the stick on the ground beside him, not in the dog's direction (test 11). After this phase of the test the judges return and once again speak to the dog in a friendly manner (test 12).

This section of the test, in which the dog is not supported by the owner, is broken off completely and at once if the dog shows great alarm or even panic.

In Section 3 the dog's sensitivity to noise is tested by judging his reaction to a couple of revolver shots (test 13).

Now takes place the 'attack' on the master by the 'criminal'. This is aimed exclusively at the dog's owner. The dog is brought forward on a long lead which is released by the master at the moment of attack (test 14). Here giving commands to the dog and encouraging him are not only expressly allowed, but are considered highly desirable.

During the test three judges make notes about the behavior shown by the dog. His reaction to environmental stimuli is described: the posture of the body, his tail and ears, whether he stands fast, advances or draws back, etc. In addition the judge notes by means of the symbols " – ", " ± ", or " + " whether the dog shows fear, with a brief explanation of the reasons for his verdict.

108

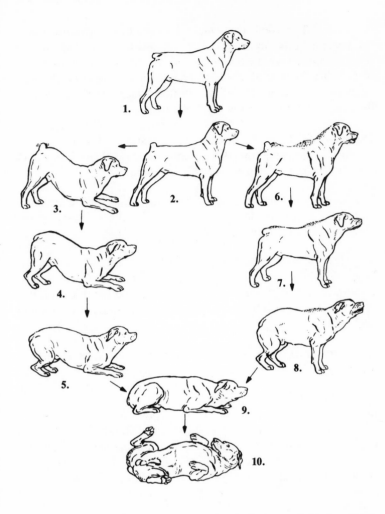

Expressive postures of the Rottweiler. 1 is the neutral posture; 2 the alert and attentive posture; 3 shows the invitation to play; 4 shows the active form of the submissive greeting (the tail is now and then depressed); 5 shows the passive form of submissive greeting (the tail is low).

The manner in which the ears are held undergoes a change, as does the weight distribution between the fore and hindquarters; 9 shows passive submission, and 10 shows this is an even more pronounced form through lying on the back and exposing the underside of the body. 6, 7 and 8 show the different stages between the aggressive posture and the ambivalent fear, defense and attack posture (after Fox).

After the test in which about eight dogs are judged (the maximum for one day) the judges arrive at an agreed assessment of the results and record their conclusions for each dog on a special form. With the help of this form and of forms containing the field notes of the judges, the full committee decides on the placing of the dog in one of the three classes - A, B or C.

These signify: Class A - suitable for breeding. Class B - not unsuitable for breeding (this large class is subdivided into B(A), B(B) and B(C). Class C - unsuitable for breeding.

The judges' conclusions and the awarded classification are communicated to the owner of the dog and to the secretary of the breeding advisory committee.

The class to which the dog is assigned depends mainly on the degree to which he shows fearlessness (absence of timidity and of avoidance and flight tendencies). In the second place attention is paid, among other things, to sharpness, jumpiness, attention and liveliness.

As a member of the committee concerned with this, I make use of a piont system in which the object is to score as low as possible.

Absence of fear gives 0 points, some fear 1 point, obvious fear 2 points. More than average or great sharpness are penalized with 2 points, since both social life and the breed standard call for less than average sharpness. Jumpiness which oversteps a certain upper limit is judged unfavorably, as is liveliness which oversteps a specific upper or lower limit; attentiveness, however, is a favorable factor.

The relationship between number of points and class are as follows:

0 - 1	A
2 - 3	B (A)
4 - 5	B (B)
6 - 7	B (C)
8	C

In borderline cases bitches are judged more leniently than dogs.

In the points system, and also in discussing the observed behavior, attention is paid exclusively to aspects of behavior which are definable, measurable, sufficiently important and not unduly influenced by environmental factors. On the latter point, flight tendencies are seldom consciously activated in the normal environment in which a dog lives. A good deal of importance can rightly be attached to this aspect of behavior.

Submissive behavior is constantly activated, though the degree to which this occurs can differ markedly.

To be obedient a dog has to submit. In what way and to what extent a dog is rendered obedient will have a strong influence on his later behavior, not only towards people but also towards others of his species. Spoiled dogs domineer over ones that have been strictly brought up. A constitutionally hard and aggressive dog can become submissive in the hands of a dominant master, and that without ever resorting to beating. Research has shown that dogs display almost the same dominance/submissive behavior outside their social group as they do within it.

A dog that 'knows' that he occupies a position in the family hierarchy far below that of the pack leader and of other people will be more likely to show submissive behavior in the test. Hence it makes little sense to pay attention to the absence of such behavior.

A dog's sharpness is not stimulated in most environments. A high degree of sharpness must be regarded with a good deal of suspicion and must exclude a dog from the highest marking or perhaps even from breeding. One often hears it said that the Rottweiler is not a dog for everybody, and that is certainly true as far as the males are concerned. Breeding with really sharp dogs makes the Rottweiler fit only for highly gifted individuals.

It is wrong to limit the qualification A to dogs that show almost perfect behavior in all respects. This implies that in addition to a very good disposition the environment must also have been good. Most environments are far from ideal. Flexibility is therefore necessary in classifying dogs. The behavior of a dog during the test should not be examined in the way that this is done by the judge at a police dog selection; as soon as he sees anything that does not please him he knocks points off. In our behavior test we do not consider whether a dog has been helped to perform a number of tasks by suitable conditioning. If one wants to get as good a picture as possible of the hereditary constitution which underlies behavior, a different approach must be chosen in which the attempt is made to eliminate a number of environmental influences. Real progress would be made in this field if all young dogs were to grow up in a standardized type of enriched environment.

Judging behavior is a subjective matter, but this does not mean that no firm line can be drawn. An improvement of the test conditions can be achieved by reducing the number of variable factors which are difficult to control. A first step along the way to a genuine measuring of behavior can be taken by the use during the test of apparatus for the measurement of heart beat, blood pressure and galvanic skin response. This will not indeed result in the complete elimination of environmental influences, the goal is increased objectivity.

The Rottweiler is a dog that, because of its docked tail and hanging ears, has rather limited scope for showing expression. This makes it desirable to use video apparatus during the test (particular situations can be shown again as often as desired). It is also possible in this way to let the owner see the dog's behavior in the second part of the test. Another method is to hold the test in open ground instead of among trees, with the owner at a great distance, out of the wind and perhaps using binoculars.

A section of this test which is considered difficult by the uninitiated and leads to misunderstanding about the method of classification is the attack. Biting the 'criminal' is seen as a necessary first step on the way to the highest qualification. Nothing is further from the truth; any Rottweiler can be taught to

Oscar van het Brabantpark (Gerlach van het Branbantpark x Onsbessy van de Brantsberg). Marked A in Dutch Rottweiler Club's behavior test. Best dog tested for behavior in 1975.

Kuno von der Lüneburgerheide (Quinto vom Kursaal x Heidi von der Lüneburgerheide).

Nina Triomfator (Pepijn x Ch. Nanjaa).

Fed. Ch. 1964 *Emir vom Freienhagen, VH III,* (Cäsar von der Frühstückstube x Afra von Freienhagen). Declared valuable for breeding by the ADRK.

Rohalt van de Beldter, VH I, (Nanthi Igor van de Brantsberg x Aife van de Molengriend). Marked B (B) in Dutch Rottweiler Club's behavior test.

Bulli vom Hause Fehsenbeck, VH III, (Berno vom Albtal x Kati vom Oelberg). Declared valuable for breeding by the ADRK.

In an environment offering sufficient space and variety, the developing senses and increasing mobility determine the extent to which the dog acquires the impressions

bite, certainly when he is on the long line and the master is close by.

A normal, steady dog which is well controlled but not conditioned to the padded jacket will not bite directly. An inexperienced dog which attacks at once is too sharp and not obedient enough. In this section of the test it is enough if the dog jumps around the struggling couple (master and 'criminal'). Some inexperienced dogs bite their master gently in the sleeve. They see what is going on as a game and prefer to play with him.

As to other parts of the test:

a. When the dog bristles in situations which do not imply any (intended) threat, this indicates insecurity and is judged unfavorably. Dogs that show this in the first part of this test generally fail completely in the second part.

b. Any dog may show fear, but it is not the intention that he should attack those handling the objects (test 5), or that in walking past the objects he should make a wide detour around them.

c. An untrained but steady dog is not expected, in the second part of the test, to launch into a serious confrontation with the 'criminal'. It is good if he does not retreat, but not bad if he quietly retreats a little.

Though some aspects of behavior are outside the scope of this test (behavior towards small children, and behavior of dogs towards bitches), a test such as this can be extremely useful for the selection of animals for breeding. It is the first step in paying attention to the behavior of the dog, which is something too important to be neglected. Inappropriate behavior by a dog in a family is the cause of much misery. Sharp and irrascible male Rottweilers can inflict serious injuries, and the grief when such a dog has to be destroyed can also be great.

Certificate of Breeding Value For a Bitch

as verified by the German Rottweiler Club (ADRK) as
having gone through the Breeding Value Test for Rottweilers.

Place: Schwarmsted
Date: 21-9-75
Judge: P. Schafer

Working Dog Breeding

Approved for Breeding:
For 2 years, until 20-9-77

Name: EDDA VOM INGENHOF   H.D. Free
Date of Birth: 4-8-71   Studbook No. 46 334   Title:SchH I

    Sire: Dux vom Stuffelkopf, 44 461, SchH III, FH
         (Igor vom Hause Henseler, 42 175, SchH III
         (Tilla von der Solitude, 41 677

    Dam: Dedda vom Kursaal, 43275, SchH I
         (Blitz vom Schloss Westerwinkel, 37 642, SchH III
         (Flora vom Kursaal, 40 526, SchH II

    Inbreeding:
Breeder: Dieter Strehlow   City: 5231 Oberolfen
Owner: Walter Genennichen   City: 5900 Siegen-Kaan-Marienborn
                              Street: Kirchtaler Weg 20

Notification of change of ownership is to be made at the studbook office within 8
days at the latest, together with this Breeding Value Certificate and fee.

New Owner: (date, day & hour)   Address:

DETERMINATION OF BREEDING VALUE

I.   **General overall appearance and condition, build and movement, structure, character and fighting instinct:**
1. *Robust, strong bone, compact, substantial, correctly built, in correct size. Beautiful, noble head with dark eyes and well-carried ears. Built without fault, angulation very good. Markings, coat correct.*
2. a) Sex characteristic: *pronounced, present.*
   b) Constitution: *robust, dry, somewhat firm, somewhat fine.*
3. Character, including condition of nerves: *lively, calm; alert, somewhat constrained, mild; bold, fearless, strong nerves & lively; a little overexcited.*
4. Expression: *Rottweiler serenity, lively, intelligent, noble somewhat unfriendly.*

II.   **Parts of the Body While Standing:**
1. Proportion: *long, somewhat long, somewhat short. Robust, too heavy, heavy, medium heavy, somewhat light, full body, sufficiently full body; stocky (compact), deep, somewhat broad, somewhat narrow, slightly slabsided; good standing.*
2. a) Height at Withers: *23 5/8 inches*
   b) Depth of Chest: *11 3/8 inches*
   c) Chest circumference: *34 1/2 inches*
   d) Length of body: *28 inches*
   e) Weight: *94 3/4 pounds*

3. a) Bone: _strong_, medium strong, somwhat gross, somewhat fine.
   b) Muscles: _strong_, sufficiently strong, _dry_.
   c) Front angulation: _very good_, good, sufficient.
   d) Rear angulation: _very good_, good, sufficient;
4. a) Coat condition: _healthy_, lustrous, in condition
   b) Type of Coat: _correct texture_, somewhat long, _coarse_, _strong_, _undercoat present_, short.
5. a) Color & Markings: _Black with brown._
   b) Pigmentation: _much_, sufficient.
6. a) Head: very strong, _strong_, somewhat weak, somewhat small, slightly shortened, slightly over long.
   a) Eye Color: _dark_, light, dark brown, light brown, yellow.
   a) Ear Carriage: high, _set to the side_, _small_, heavy.
   b) Depth of Muzzle: _good_, still adequate, full, long, too small.
   c) Jaw Structure: _scissors bite_.
   d) Bite: _healthy_, _strong_, somewhat weak, partly discolored.

III. Movement in Walk & Trot (on & off leash):
Trot: _springy_, _covering much ground_, far-reaching, level back in movement.
Set of Elbows: _very good_, good, sufficient,
hackeny movement, slightly cowhocked, slightly bowlegged;
good, sufficiently _strong front foot joint_;
good, sufficiently _strong hock joint_;
Rear drive: _efficient_, sufficiently efficient, somewhat restricted.
Front movement: _very good_, good, adequate.
Tends to pace.

IV. Special Qualities of Build or Faults of Build (further remarks to section I, 1):
Build without fault, beautiful, broad head.

V. Assessment of Character (not of performance): The finding is not rated by means of declared value as excellent, good, etc., rather to underline what the condition is.

1. Character & Condition of Nerves
   a) Character: _solid_, _natural_, spirited, calm.
   b) Attentiveness: _present_, alert, _constant_.
   c) Condition of nerves: _solid_, slightly overexcited.
   d) Openness: _present_, sufficient.
   e) Self Confidence in Crowd: _present_, sufficient.
   f) Reaction to Gunshot: _present_, sufficient.

2. Courage & Sharpness:
   a) Fighting instinct: _pronounced_, present.
   b) Courage: _pronounced_, present.
   c) Sharpness: _pronounced_, present.

3. Rating of Performance Test

Advice for Choice of Breeding Partners (Recommendations & Warnings):

Location of Test: **Date of Test:**

Judge: **Verification of ADRK Studbook Office.**

A.D.R.K.

Place: 439 Gladbeck
Date: 10 November 1973
Judge: W. Hedtke

Results of the Zuchttauglichkeitsprüfung
(Breed Suitability Test)

for ~~the dog~~ the bitch   EDDA VOM INGENHOF

Date of birth: 4, Aug. 1971   Studbook No: 46.334

Sire: Dux vom Stuffelkopf, 44 461, SchH I

Dam: Dedda vom Kursaal, 43 275, SchH I

Breeder: Dieter Strehlow, 5231 Oberölfen - Altenkirchen

Owner: Heidi & Walter Genennichen, Siegen - Kaan

Body Measurements

Height at Withers: 23 5/8 in.   Depth of Chest: 11 3/8 in.

Length of Back: 27 1/8 in.   Circumference of Chest: 33 in.

I.   Appearance & Condition, Build & Movement:

A spirited aggressive self-confident bitch of outstanding type, deep and broad substantial bitch in correct size, with strong bone and good feet. Very good bitch head, with dark eyes and small well-carried ears. Angulation correct, harsh coat, good markings. Back level and firm, farreaching movement. Tight scissors bite.

II.   Character:

Lively, alert, indifferent to gunshot, good protective and fighting spirit.

Suitable for breeding   —   ~~Not suitable~~   —   ~~Return in 6 months~~

(strike out where not applicable)

Signature of judge:

W. Hedtke

Completed form of a judgment on suitability for breeding (German Rottweiler Club A.D.R.K)

It is necessary to breed exclusively with dogs that have undergone a behavior test with a satisfactory result.

It is a pity that many Rottweiler breeders who are successful at shows care little about the behavior of their breeding animals; they prefer not to appear at tests. The photographs in this book show that there are laudable exceptions to this.

The assessment of Rottweiler behavior by the A.D.R.K.

Both the test of suitability and the test of value for breeding by the Rottweiler Club in the Federal Republic make provision for the testing of behavior.

In the test of suitability there is an assault (the owner is free to choose whether the dog is on the lead or not), the dog must then attack and receive two not too heavy blows on the back with a stick.

The dog's master stands some distance away and the dog must hold his ground. If he does not attack or if he lets go and allows himself to be chased off, he is declared 'unsuitable'.

In the second part of this test the dog, at a distance of about 40 meters from his master, must bring a running man to a standstill (the so-called 'stellen'). The 'criminal' first runs away and then turns as the dog draws near and rushes at him. The dog must bite once again. He is not really struck, but the stick is brandished over him. The master remains standing some way off; the dog may let go after the first onset but must remain with the 'criminal'.

After that the dog is put on the lead and a shot is fired at a distance of 25 meters. The dog must not show fear.

The test of value (the 'Körung') includes the following. Master and dog walk through a group of people who clap their hands. The dog should not react aggressively. Since he has first received the comand, 'Heel', this is no problem. Then, after leaving the group, a shot is fired at a distance of about 15 meters.

In the second part of this test the dog must 'quarter'. This involves searching the whole area for the man in the padded jacket who has concealed himself somewhere. Having found him, the dog should bark at him and so make known where the 'criminal' has hidden himself. In this situation there is no objection if the dog doees not bark but instead momentarily attacks. The master now comes up and calls the dog off, or tries to. The 'criminal' emerges from the bushes and the dog should take a firm grip on him and detain him. The dog is often dragged along for a distance of 15 meters. When the 'criminal' stands still the dog receives the command, 'Leave'. The dog that obeys this command now comes off worse than the one that ignores it; there follows a direct attack by the 'criminal' on the dog. The 'criminal' rushes at the dog from a distance of several meters; the dog must once again take a firm grip and, having done so, must continually leap backwards to avoid having his paws trampled on or pulling the man on top of him. This is followed by two severe blows (I have seen cases in which this resulted in a cane as thick as one's thumb being broken). The dog may let go for a fraction of a second and must then at once attack again. If he lets go and stays, or if he lets go and runs away, he is judged to be 'not valuable for Rottweiler breeding'.

The test concludes with the 'long pursuit'. The dog must 'stellen' at a distance of about 70 meters from his master. Dog and 'criminal' once again rush towards each other and in this confrontation the dog again receives two blows with the stick. Here, too, the dog must clearly bite and hold fast.

In the 'Körung' a distinction is drawn between dogs and bitches; the latter are not hit as hard.

Comparison between the Dutch and German test

The ADRK assumes that the dog is trained. The Dutch Rottweiler Club test can be taken by both trained and untrained dogs; this has no influence on the end result. The percentage of trained dogs that fail tests 9, 10 and 11 is no different from the percentage of untrained dogs.

Nothing is gained when being trained is a prerequisite for taking part in a test. Behavior is the result of interaction between inherited disposition and environment. The more emphasis is placed on the presence of correct environmental influences, the greater is the danger that the inherited disposition will be obscured.

It is doubtful whether the test of suitability has much value in the cases in which a dog is allowed to take this test on his own ground and with a 'criminal' who is already known to him. In a good behavior test the dog is confronted with unfamiliar things and is brought into novel situations. There is not much point in getting a dog to work through known programs, particularly as there is no way of knowing how much time has been spent in training him for it. Some dogs do not need to be taught to stand up to a test, while others learn quickly and others again take years. I well remember an Alsatian with a bad disposition (very timid and nervous at 2 months old) who won a police dog certificate at the fourth attempt when he was 7 years old (after some 6 years of training). On the previous occasions he had run away from the stick. It is wrong to say that this dog is valuable for breeding because he has the certificate.

It is the energy, dedication and patience of the owner that got him the certificate despite, rather than thanks to the natural disposition of the dog. However, it rarely happens that German Rottweilers pass the 'Körung' in this fashion. Many dogs fail, not because of lack of aptitude, but because of the hard and brutal training that has gone before. Many trainers think that a Rottweiler cannot be broken mentally and use harsh measures. Many German Rottweilers are subdued in the presence of their owners. There is scarcely a master/dog relationship, at least not in a positive sense. The relationship is a loveless one; the dog is almost never a household pet and has no experience of people. This emotional inadequacy is an enormous handicap in such a severe and difficult test. The merit of the test of value lies in the fact that when dogs have survived such an unfortunate environment without noticeable damage and then pass the test at a relatively early age (before the fourth year), it can be assumed that their hereditary disposition is good. The same cannot be said with equal certainty of dogs which pass and have a good relationship with their owner (especially if they are somewhat older).

In recent years Rottweiler bitches have been relatively more successful in the test of value than the dogs. The fact that they are more discreetly handled, spend more time in the house and later form a bond with their master, is likely to have a good deal to do with it. An inherent drawback of the test of value is that excessive sharpness and irascibility are rarely revealed and are therefore not penalized.

The Dutch Rottweiler Club test is more closely in tune with the developments that have taken place in recent years in the scientific study of behavior. Moreover a dog can take part in it without his owner being expected to have spent time in training. The test has more affinity with the dog's normal activities, and the result yields a more finely shaded picture. Another big difference; arises from the fact that the Dutch test also assesses the behavior of the dog when his master is not present. Much of the conditioning to which the dog has been subjected is left behind in the second part of the test. This part is all the more important because it is there that particularly big differences in behavior appear.

A test has little point if almost all dogs perform it either well or very badly; it has a lot of point if a whole scale of behavior patterns is observed. This occurs in this part of the test; some dogs try to run away in utter panic, some do not budge an inch, and all variations in between.

One of the striking things about it is that this behavior seems to have a clear hereditary basis. Descendants of *Cuno vom Hause Kommelt* generally do well in this part (and in the reaminder of the tests), as do those of *Moritz vom Silahopp* (two imported dogs). Descendants of *Arras van de Barrot* show the opposite very clearly.

The Rottweiler behavior test in Finland

In Scandinavia and Finland there are many Rottweilers and various Rottweiler clubs, all of which subject their dogs to a behavior test. The differences between these tests are small. To illustrate the test methods used in Northern Europe, a short description is given here of the Finnish behavior test.

One of the good sides is that this test too judges an excess of sharpness unfavorably. This emerges from the way in which marks are awarded not only for sharpness as such, but also for the display of extreme fanaticism in the defense of the master and for lack of 'sociability' (aggression).

During the test the dog wears a collar and is kept on the lead by his owner or tied to a tree. He is at least 18 months old and not trained.

a. The dog is led right past a tree, at the moment of passing, a metal bucket full of stones and empty tins falls down. The noise is increased by dropping the bucket on to the edge of a large metal tray lying upside down. The dog's reaction is observed when the bucket hits the tray and the ground. After master and dog have walked around the tree, the dog should react by sniffing at the bucket without showing fear.

b. The master holds his dog on a long lead, and both stand still. A sled on which a life-sized dummy sits is pulled from behind a screen in the dog's direction. This is done slowly, with many stops, until finally a strong jerk is given, causing the sled to fall over.

    The owner then walks up to the sled, allows the dog to sniff at it and reassures him. Both walk 20 paces away, turn around and walk past the sled without stopping. The dog, at first excited by the sled, should show no unease on the way back.

c. The dog is tied to a tree with a line about 1.25 meters long; his owner disappears out of sight. At a short distance from the tree there is - invisible to the dog - a man behind a haystack who fires revolver shots on both sides of the haystack. After the last shot has been fired, the man appears from his hiding place and approaches the dog with the judge. The dog should display no aggression or fear towards either of them.

d. The owner walks at a normal speed with his dog on a long lead past a tractor. A 'criminal' with a padded sleve on one arm and a rolled up jute sack in the other hand jumps out from behind the tractor and hits the owner with the sack.

The dog should stop the 'criminal' from doing this. If the dog does not display this reaction, the 'criminal' grabs the owner by the shoulders and shakes him to and fro.

The overall method of awarding marks, with some examples, is as follows. Marks are given from $+3$ to -3.

1. Tenacity, weighted 15;

2. Sharpness, weighted 1. A high degree of sharpness is marked unfavorably;

3. Defending instinct, weighted 1. A reasonable amount of this is marked high, provided the dog displays a certain self-control. -3 is given for a very strong defensive instinct in which the dog completely loses its head;

4. Combativeness, weighted 10;

5. Steadiness, weighted 35
   $+3$: calm and self-confident (not apathetic)
   -3: very nervous behavior, gun-shy, nervous barking;

6. Temperament, weighted 15
   $+3$: lively
   $+2$: fairly lively
   $+1$: very lively;

7. Hardness, weighted 8;

8. Sociability, weighted 15
   -3: aggressive or very reserved behavior.

The points are added together and divided by 100 (the total of the weight factors). The result is a number to one place of decimals.

Weighted Average	Conclusion
+3.0 – 2.5	Very suitable for breeding
+2.4 – 1.5	Suitable
+1.4 – 0.0	Reasonably suitable
−0.1 – 1.5	Less Suitable
−1.6 – 2.5	Unsuitable
−2.6 – 3.0	Completely unsuitable